Essays in Real Estate Research

Band 14

Edited by
N. B. Rottke, Eschborn, Germany
J. Mutl, Wiesbaden, Germany

Die Reihe „Essays in Real Estate Research", herausgegeben von Professor Dr. Nico B. Rottke FRICS und Professor Jan Mutl, Ph.D. umfasst aktuelle Forschungsarbeiten der Promovenden der Lehrstühle und Professuren des Real Estate Management Institutes der EBS Business School. Forschungs- und Lehrschwerpunkte des Institutes bilden die interdisziplinären Aspekte der Immobilientransaktion sowie die nachhaltige Wertschöpfungskette im Immobilienlebenszyklus. Die Kapitalmärkte werden als essenzieller Bestandteil der Entwicklung der Immobilienmärkte aufgefasst.
Die in der Regel empirischen Studien betrachten transaktions- und kapitalmarktnahe Themenbereiche aus dem Blickwinkel der institutionellen Immobiliengewerbe- und -wohnungswirtschaft, wie bspw. Finanzierung, Kapitalmarktstruktur, Investition, Risikomanagement, Bewertung, Ökonomie oder Portfoliomanagement, aber auch angewandte Themen wie Corporate Real Estate Management, Projektentwicklung oder Unternehmensführung. Die ersten 11 Bände der Reihe erschienen bis 2014 auch im Immobilien Manager Verlag, Köln.

The series "Essays in Real Estate Research", published by Professor Dr. Nico B. Rottke FRICS and Professor Jan Mutl, Ph.D., includes current research work of doctoral students at the chairs and professorships of the Real Estate Management Institute of EBS Business School. The research and teaching focus of the Institute constitutes the interdisciplinary aspects of real estate transactions as well as the sustainable value creation chain within the real estate life cycle. The capital markets are regarded as essential components of the development of the real estate markets. The mostly empirical studies consider transactional as well as capital market topics from the point of view of the institutional commercial and residential real estate industry, such as finance, capital market structure, investment, risk management, valuation, economics or portfolio management, but also applied topics such as corporate real estate management, real estate development, or leadership issues in the property industry. The first 11 volumes of the series appeared up until 2014 in Immo-bilien Manager Publishing, Cologne, as well.

Edited by

Prof. Dr. Nico B. Rottke
Ernst & Young Real Estate GmbH
Eschborn, Germany

Jan Mutl
EBS Business School
Wiesbaden, Germany

More information about this series at http://www.springer.com/series/13911

Holger Markmann

Covered Bonds under Unconventional Monetary Policy

With a Foreword by Professor Dr. Nico B. Rottke and Professor Jan Mutl, PhD

Springer Gabler

Holger Markmann
Wiesbaden, Deutschland

Doctoral Thesis, EBS Business School, EBS Universität für Wirtschaft und Recht, Wiesbaden, Germany, 2017

Essays in Real Estate Research
ISBN 978-3-658-20974-2 ISBN 978-3-658-20975-9 (eBook)
https://doi.org/10.1007/978-3-658-20975-9

Library of Congress Control Number: 2018932746

Springer Gabler

Printed on acid-free paper

This Springer Gabler imprint is published by the registered company
Springer Fachmedien Wiesbaden GmbH part of Springer Nature
The registered company address is: Abraham-Lincoln-Str. 46, 65189 Wiesbaden, Germany

To all bright and loving people in my life.

Foreword

You are in the priviliged situation to have chosen the present work of Dr. Holger Markmann as a source of information on covered bonds, the financial crisis, and the European Central Bank's interventions in the respective market. Independent of your level of comfort with the topics under consideration, the present work constitutes a detailed overview of the basics required to comprehend theses complex markets and and is able to advance into providing coherent results on the effectiveness of the European Central Bank's actions.

The author is able to demonstrate rigorous analyses on the covered bond markets and argues that the first Covered Bond Purchase Programme has been successful, while the second and third programs suffer from deficiencies in their timing and target definition. He therefore derives conclusions about the likelihood of a future implementation of Covered Bond Purchase Programmes, which may surprise or not be in line with the default opinion of parts of the audience of this work. Nonetheless, it remaining committed to academic independence and excellence, the work pays tribute to Humboldt's dictum of academia's independence, regardless of social, political, or economical forces.

The work, therefore, provides a great fit for the series 'Essays in Real Estate Research', which aims to provide state-of-the-art research in real estate and its interdisciplinary aspects. As editors, we are pleased to welcome this work in the series, fostering its interdisciplinary competencies in the fields of real estate financing and monetary policy. We finally hope for and are confident for this hightly relevant work to be well received in academia and industry.

Professor Dr. Nico B. Rottke
Professor Jan Mutl, PhD

Preface

The past decade was one studded with radical economic and financial developments and changes in the banking landscape, monetary policy, and the economic state in the Eurozone. In these times, the rather boring bank funding tool of covered bonds has presented the 'go-to'-instrument for unconventional monetary policy. I am thankful for being able to provide a valuable academic contribution to the fascinating developments in times of the global financial crisis and the European sovereign debt crisis. Thus, I am in high hopes to provide insightful knowldge for future Monetary Policy setting and to provide covered bond markets with a more fomalized understanding of the interventions in their market. It additionally sets the stage for further, even more holistic research on unconventional monetary policy and its implications on industries, such as real estate.

It is an honour to express my sincerest gratitude to my first supervisor Professor Nico B. Rottke for his continuous support, the opportunities provided, and his great leadership. I also thank my second supervisor Professor Ferdinand Mager, and Professors Jan Mutl and Joachim Zietz for their relentless help with initially grueling econometrics and academic conventions. However, it is Professor Heidi Falkenbach, who I hold accountable for turning my thinking and acting into that of an academic.

It was a priviledge to work with the greatly spirited team of EBS REMI, which has a truly outstanding capacity, but is more importantly a place rich of amazing people. I am grateful for the time spent with Professor John Glascock and his team at the University of Connecticut and for his proving the best environment I could have asked for to finalize the work at hand.

The biggest thanks go to my family for their dedication and support on multiple levels in me thriving for my dreams and aspirations. Finally, I am to recognize Ms Astrid Schmitz for bearing the largest load and making the biggest sacrifices, while remaining warmhearted all throughout—thank you!

Dr. Holger Markmann

Table of Contents

List of Figures

List of Tables

List of Abbreviations

ABSPP	Asset Backed Securities Purchase Programme
ARMAX	Autoregressive–Moving-Average Model with Exogenous Inputs
bp	Basis Point
Bunds	German sovereign bonds
CBPP	Covered Bond Purchase Programme
EAPP	Extended Asset Purchase Programme
EBA	European Banking Authority
ECB	European Central Bank
EFSM	European Financial Stability Mechanism
EMF	European Mortgage Federation
ESFF	European Financial Stability Facility
ESM	European Stability Mechanism
FRFA	Fixed-Rate Tender, Full Allotment
GARCH	Generalized Autoregressive Conditional Heteroskedasticity
GARCH-M	Generalized Autoregressive Conditional Heteroskedasticity in Mean
GFC	Global Financial Crisis
Gilts	British sovereign bonds
HQLA	High Quality Liquid Assets
IID	Independent and Identically Distributed
IMF	International Monetary Fund
IPSI	Italy, Portugal, Spain, and Ireland
LCR	Liquidity Coverage Ratio
LSAP	Large-Scale Asset Purchases
LTRO	Longer-Term Refinancing Operations
LTV	Loan-to-Value
MBS	Mortgage Backed Securities
MRO	Main Refinancing Operations
NSFR	Net Stable Funding Ratio
OIS	Overnight Indexed Swap
OMT	Outright Monetary Transactions

PSPP	Public Sector Purchase Programme
QE	Quantitative Easing
SMP	Securities Markets Programme
SPV	Special Purpose Vehicle
TIPS	Treasury Inflation Protected Securities
TLTRO	Targeted Longer-Term Refinancing Operation
UCITS	Undertakings for Collective Investments in Transferable Securities
UCM	Unobserved Components Model
VAR	Vector-Autoregression
VSTOXX	Eurostoxx 50 Volatility Index

1 Introduction

The European Central Bank (ECB) found covered bonds to be of the utmost importance for a functioning European banking system. As this market had become largely dysfunctional after the onset of the global financial crisis (GFC), the ECB initiated its first Covered Bond Purchase Programme (CBPP1) in May 2009. These outright bond purchases were among the first unconventional monetary policy measures of the ECB, after reaching the zero lower bound.[1] Having initially succeeded at revitalizing the covered bond market, the Eurosystem[2] conducted two further Covered Bond Purchase Programmes (CBPP2 and CBPP3), holding an aggregate €129 billion in covered bonds per June 2015 (ECB, 2015a).

Further unconventional monetary policy measures include the outright sovereign bond purchases from Greece, Ireland, and Portugal, as part of the Securities Markets Programme (SMP) in 2010, and its reactivation in the following year to purchase Italian and Spanish sovereign bonds. In aggregate, the Eurosystem held bonds totaling €218 billion under the SMP per December 2012 (ECB, 2013). Replacing the SMP, the Outright Monetary Transactions (OMT) program was introduced in 2012, but not activated to date. Finally, in 2015, the Eurosystem engaged its Public Sector Purchase Programme (PSPP), under which it held €205 billion per June 2015 (ECB, 2015a).

The Literature on the Eurosystem's sovereign bond purchases was able to build on previous works on the quantitative easing (QE) measures undertaken by the Bank of Japan, the Federal Reserve, and the Bank of England. Focusing on the SMP, they find a yield compression, confirming its effectiveness in line with the ECB's objective of easing capital market funding for its member countries through a tighter interest term structure (e.g., Falagiarda & Reitz, 2015; Eser & Schwab, 2015).

---

[1] Zero lower bound refers to the assumption that the central bank interest rate cannot be lowered beyond zero, whereby the main monetary policy tool for setting short-term interest rates diminishes. Refer to Section 3 for details.

[2] *Eurosystem* refers to the national central banks and the European Central Bank, which are responsible for the European monetary policy. Its operations are *ex officio* administered by the various units of the European Central Bank.

H. Markmann, *Covered Bonds under Unconventional Monetary Policy*,
Essays in Real Estate Research 14,
https://doi.org/10.1007/978-3-658-20975-9_1

Contrary, literature has not yet exhaustively determined the effectiveness of the three CBPPs. Beirne et al. (2011), Szczerbowicz (2015), and Gibson, Hall, and Tavlas (2015) analyze CBPP1 and CBPP2. They find the programs to have led to tighter covered bond spreads.[3] In addition, Beirne et al. (2011) analyze primary market effects and find a crowding out of senior unsecured bonds in favor of covered bonds during CBPP1.

Building on these works, we[4] expand the literature on the Eurosystem's CBPPs. We contribute by analyzing the effectiveness of all three CBPPs on covered bond markets, employing rigorous difference-in-difference estimations, extending the scope of relevant unconventional monetary policy announcements, and considering the primary market impact. We further analyze our results on the grounds of the ECB's unconventional monetary policy regime and the changing macro-economic circumstances.

The structure of this work is as follows: In Sections 2 and 3, we lay the basis for the empirical analysis herein. The former introduces the covered bond market, focusing on its function for bank funding, providing an overview on the investor universe and the structure of primary and secondary covered bond markets. The latter focuses on the transmission mechanism of unconventional monetary policy, its implementation by the ECB through time, and outright covered bond purchase programs conducted in other currency areas. Sections 4 to 6 present empirical analyses of the impact of the Eurosystem's covered bond purchases on the primary and secondary covered bond markets. They provide insights to the questions presented from different angles of analysis (Table 1).

In detail, Section 4 analyzes whether CBPP1 to CBPP3 have led to an increased emission volume of covered bonds. We embed a difference-in-difference analysis within a quarterly panel fixed effects model to determine emission volumes in excess of those of a comparable control group.

Section 5, shifts focus to the secondary market and we analyze the impact of the announcement and implementation of the three CBPPs on eurozone covered bond indexes, compared to that of the United Kingdom. Our unobserved compo-

---

3 Several spreads are referred to throughout the analysis. Wider (tighter) spreads refer to an increasing (decreasing) difference between the two rates. If not specified differently, we refer to the spread versus the asset swap rate. Refer to Section 2.4.2 for details.

4 For consistency and ease of comprehension, the first person plural is used entirely throughout the document. Whenever Sections are co-authored, this is explicitly mentioned.

nents model with weekly observations allows us to determine the duration of CBPP announcement effects.

Table 1: Overview of Research Sections

	Section 4) Impact on Emission Activity	Section 5) Medium-term Impact on the Secondary Market	Section 6) Short-term Announcement Impact on the Secondary Market
Research Setup			
Market Segment	Primary	Secondary	Secondary
Subject	Covered Bond Emission Volume	Covered Bond Yield Spread vs. United Kingdom	Covered Bond Yield Spread vs. Asset Swap
Methodology	Panel Fixed Effects	Unobserved Components Model	Panel Random Effects
Control Group	Denmark, Norway, Sweden, United Kingdom	United Kingdom	Canada, Norway, Sweden, United Kingdom, United States
Data			
Level	Country	Country	Individual Bond
Source	Thomson Reuters SDC Platinum	Markit iBoxx	Thomson Reuters Datastream
Frequency	Quarterly	Weekly	Daily

Source: Own illustration

Remaining in the realm of secondary market analysis, Section 6 focuses on the announcement effects of a broad array of unconventional monetary policy instruments on covered bond spreads. In order to draw specific conclusions, we employ a panel random effects model on the individual covered bond level and draw our conclusions from a broad control group of non-eurozone countries.

Combining the previous literature and the results gained through our own analysis, we infer implications for the future use of outright covered bond purchases, considering different economic conditions in Section 7. Finally, Section 8 concludes.

2 Covered Bond Market

Covered bonds are a sub-category of corporate bonds. They are different in that they are collateralized by high quality loans, which are ring-fenced to provide covered bond investors a preferential claim in case of an issuer default. As only financial institutions possess a sufficient volume of loans, covered bonds present a special funding vehicle for financial institutions.[5]

2.1 Background

Generally, covered bonds may be collateralized by high quality loans. As this terminology is not exhaustive, there exist different asset classes, which are considered sufficiently safe for their use as covered bond collateral. These differ depending on the legislation a covered bond is issued under. Most typically, mortgages and public sector loans are considered such high quality, yet subject to further regulatory requirements. While mortgages are collateralized by a real asset, public sector covered bonds are ultimately expected to be guaranteed by the sovereign, which provides the lowest risk possible.[6] Further, loans may also be collateralized by ships (France), airplanes (Germany), or art (Austria).

In addition to being collateralized by high quality loans, covered bonds exhibit a number of further properties, making them a very safe debt instrument. The foremost is its dual recourse structure. This refers to the fact, that all loans serving for collateral in a covered bond have to be 'ring-fenced', that is they can be serviced and generate income, independently of the lender institution's going concern. The entirety of these loans is called a cover pool. In the case of the lender institution's default, bond investors have a first claim on the ring-fenced loans and all proceeds from their servicing, which provides a first recourse. If the before mentioned claim is not sufficient, investors may claim a second, *pari*

---

[5] Refer to Grossmann and Stöcker (2016), Larsson (2013), and Schwarcz (2011) for more extensive introductions to covered bonds in general and Spangler and Werner (2014) for German Pfandbriefs in particular.

[6] We are aware that this view has been largely challenged since the onset of the GFC, yet the rationale ramains intact.

H. Markmann, *Covered Bonds under Unconventional Monetary Policy*,
Essays in Real Estate Research 14,
https://doi.org/10.1007/978-3-658-20975-9_2

passu recourse from the lender's assets.[7] On the other hand, the loans of the cover pool may not be utilized to settle any general claims before all covered bond investors' claims are satisfied.

Secondly, most jurisdictions only allow for a fraction, in terms of loan-to-value (LTV), of the cover loans to serve as collateral for cover pool purposes. The limits imposed herein differ by country, typically ranging from 60%, such as in Germany[8] to 80%. The most common separation is 60% LTV for commercial and 80% LTV for residential loans.

Thirdly, covered bond issuers are required to maintain the quality of the cover pool. This takes place by means of replacing amortized or delinquent loans with new high quality loans. A third party managing the cover pool and rating agencies, monitor the cover pool quality, and the level of 'over-collateralization'.[9] The sum of these properties makes covered bonds bankruptcy remote, leading to conservative risk-return profile.

The exact provisions and thereby the safety measures are either set by the bond's or bond program's prospectus, or proclaimed by the legislation under which a covered bond is issued. The first is called a 'structured covered bond', while the latter is called a 'legislative covered bond'. Independent of its legal status, covered bonds are generally structured to provide the largest benefit to the issuer and its investors. While this is mostly done via the coupon rate for publicly traded covered bonds, there is room for further parameter changes, such as the maturity, or interest structure.[10] Private placements, allow for greater flexibility, such as in optionality, or the quality of the collateral.

With the oldest covered bonds dating back to 1770,[11] only Denmark (1851), Germany (1900), Switzerland (1931), and Spain (1982) had introduced covered bond legislation pre-1990. Thereafter, a number of countries, including France and central European countries followed in the mid-1990s with another wave

---

7 Hillenbrand (2013) points out that the intrinsic value of the secondary recourse is negligible if the issuer is a specialized emissions bank, as would be the case for example, for French legislative covered bonds.

8 Based on the German concept of 'Lending Value' (dt. Beleihungswert) instead of the LTV.

9 Obtaining a rating is not required for private placements, i.e. covered bonds not trading in capital markets.

10 We abstain from introducing 'Soft-Bullet' and 'Pass-Through' structures. For details, see Hillenbrand (2013) and Rudolf and Rühlmann (2016).

11 See Larsson (2013) for a brief history of covered bonds, as well as the considerations brought forward introducing them to the United States, particularly a comparison to MBS.

arriving in the 2000s. Parts of the latter were countries, such as the United Kingdom, Austria, Italy, Greece, and Portugal. Further non-European countries with covered bond legislature include the United States, Japan, Australia, and New Zealand (Grossmann & Stöcker, 2016).

With the gradual implementation into national law, countries tailored the code to their legal and economic system, resulting in very different frameworks. As the functionality of corporate bonds does not vary largely, covered bonds generally operate in the same fashion, unless the lender or the cover pool defaults. The differences are therefore largely in the frameworks' insolvency treatment, which can generally be categorized into four groups (Table 2). The differences are mainly in the requirement to establish an independent banking entity, which owns the loans and issues the covered bonds, but has no own staff (e.g., France); an abstract and only nominal separation of the cover pool (e.g., Germany); and a 'true sale' of the loans to a special purpose vehicle (SPV), which in turn guarantees the interest and principle payments of the covered bonds emitted by the lender (Hillenbrand, 2013).

With the growing number of frameworks, and further integrating capital markets, there are tendencies for a harmonization of European covered bond frameworks, which are also promoted by the European Banking Authority (2016). However, due to the long standing history and resilience of some of these markets and the great difference between insolvency categories, there exists considerable resistance.[12]

Per end of 2015, the global covered bond market reached a volume of €2.5 trillion in outstanding bonds, of which approximately 64% are denominated in euro, 63% are benchmark bonds,[13] and 83% are backed by mortgages (European Covered Bonds Council [ECBC], 2016). During the course of the past decade, the covered bond market has undergone changes, which can be summarized by the following trends:

---

[12] For details and the current progress on the harmonization of covered bond legislation, refer to Batchvarov, Caris, and Beaumont (2016).

[13] Outstanding volume of €500 million and above

Table 2: European Covered Bond Regimes in Insolvency

	France	Denmark	Germany	Netherlands
Secondary Countries	Ireland, Norway	Luxembourg	Spain, Austria, Belgium, Spain, Portugal, Sweden	Italy, United Kingdom
Emission Banks	Yes	No	No	No
Key Characteristics	Cover pool is a specialized emission bank	← mix →	Cover pool is integrated in universal bank	Loans are 'sold' to subsidiary, guaranteeing covered bond
Advantage(s)	Cover pool is segregated; central bank access	← mix →	Valuable secondary recourse	
Disadvantage(s)	In itself not operational; no value of secondary recourse	← mix →	No central bank access; cover pool has to be segregated	Informing borrowers on sale; no central bank access

Source: Own Illustration based on Hillenbrand (2013)

In line with the introduction of new covered bond legislation, the total amount of covered bonds outstanding has increased until 2013, when it peaked at approximately €2.8 trillion (ECBC, 2016; Figure 1). This growth has been particularly strong for non-eurozone countries, which, with few exceptions, did not have covered bond legislations before.

The mostly mature covered bond markets in core European countries on the contrary, exhibit diminished volumes of covered bonds outstanding. Most of this decrease can be attributed to the decreasing importance of public sector covered bonds.[14] Their share dropped from 53% to 15% between 2005 and 2015 (Figure 2). For Germany alone they dropped from 75% to 47% in the same period (ECBC, 2016). The market therefore now mostly constitutes of mortgage covered bonds.

[14] The diminishing importance is driven by decreasing margins in the public finance sector due to decreasing financing costs for government agencies, which next to other reasons lead to the major players, such as WestLB and Hypo Real Estate exiting the market.

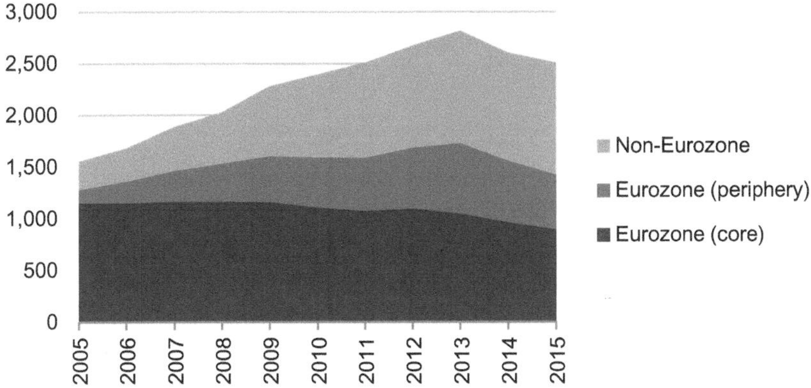

Figure 1: Outstanding Covered Bond Volume by Region
Covered bond volume is depicted in euro-billion. The periphery eurozone comprises of Cyprus, Greece, Ireland, Italy, Portugal, and Spain. Source: ECBC (2016)

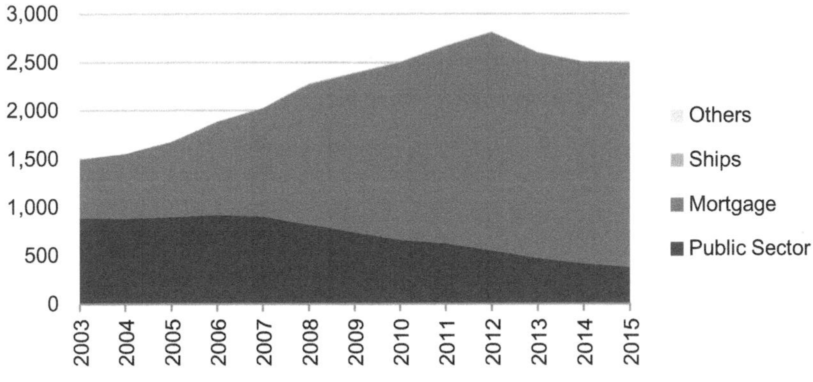

Figure 2: Outstanding Covered Bond Volume by Collateral Type
Covered bond volume is depicted in euro-billion. Source: ECBC (2016)

2.2 Supply through Bank Funding

As per year end 2016, 434 banks had implemented covered bond programs, of which a total of 314 issuers had already emitted covered bonds (ECBC, 2016). They propose a funding ability to banks, which due to its low risk profile, is inexpensive and allows for a customized asset liability management, as maturities can be varied. As such, covered bonds also provide a tool to achieve the resilience measures lined out by the recent regulation, such as the liquidity coverage ratio (LCR) and the net stable funding ratio (NSFR).

2.2.1 Comparison to MBS and Senior Unsecured

The closest substitutes to covered bonds are senior unsecured bonds and Mortgage Backed Securities (MBS). In comparison to the first, covered bonds are characterized by the additional collateral. While we have elaborated on advantages above, this enhancement feature comes at the cost of asset encumbrance[15] and the requirement to maintain a cover pool with all inherent duties.

The differentiating characteristics of MBS against covered bonds are based in their fixed asset pool, and character of a sale, leading to an issuer capital relief. The advantages of MBS over covered bonds are constituted in the foregone requirement to maintain the quality of the collateral pool, and depending on the business model, the cash-inflow upon sale. On the other hand, reporting duties are extensive. The pricing of both products depends on numerous factors, which may lead to an advantage of either one, depending on the exact specifications under consideration (International Monetary Fund, 2011). See Table 3 for an overview of the differences between all three funding products.

[15] Asset encumbrance is the term describing the diminishing asset base available for unsecured bond holders in case of a bank default, due to collateral not being able to satisfy investor claims. In terms of covered bonds, cover pool assets are not able to meet unsecured investor's claims. The larger the portion of the cover pool versus the banks total assets, the more severe becomes asset encumbrance. However, asset encumbrance can also occur due to repos or other forms of collateralization. See Stöcker (2012) for details on asset encumbrance in a covered bond setting and Houben and Slingenberg (2013) for an evaluation in general terms.

Table 3: Overview of Bank Funding Instruments

	Senior Unsecured Debt	Covered Bond: Special Law	Covered Bond: General Law	Mortgage Backed Securities (MBS)
Issuer	Lender	Lender		Special Purpose Vehicle
Payments	Lender	Lender (until insolvency)		
Preferential Claim on Collateral	No	Yes		Yes
Residual Recourse to Issuer	After all secured/other claims	Yes		No
Payment Acceleration	On issuer default	On issuer of cover pool default		On specific Event(s) ('triggers')
Collateral Pool Dynamics	No dedicated pool of collateral	Typically dynamic; issuer must maintain quality and size of cover pool		Typically static but issuer can sometimes add assets
Collateral Definition	n/a	Regulation	Regulation/ Contract	Contract
Source of Repayment	Operating cashflow	Bondholders ranking *pari passu* among each other and have a preferential claim on cover pool		Securitized assets
Asset-Liability Management	n/a	Regulation	Regulation/ Contract	Typically pass-through
Repayment Structure	Typically bullet	Typically bullet but potentially soft bullet structure		Amortizing
Issuer Capital Relief	No	No		Yes
Disclosure Requirement	Light to none	Light to none		Heavy

Source: International Monetary Fund (2011)

2.2.2 Emission Motives

Banks' emission motives for covered bonds, beyond the provision of cheap funding, are scarcely reflected upon. The contrary is the case for MBS. Literature has identified motives in the fields of liquidity and funding, credit risk management, profit enhancement, and regulatory capital arbitrage for securitization.

While regulatory capital arbitrage is not feasible under Basel II and there is transmission mechanism for credit risk (Packer, Stever, & Upper, 2007),[16] the other two options seem feasible.

Covered bond emissions provide for a cash inflow in return for future interest and principle payments. As shown by Loutskina (2011), banks are able to maintain lower levels of liquid assets, when they are able to quickly convert mortgages into liquidity through the emissions of MBS.[17] In fact, Carbo-Valverde, Rosen, & Rodríguez-Fernández (2011) are able to confirm liquidity to be a driver for covered bonds emission. There is no empirical evidence for profit enhancement motives in covered bond emissions.

Until mid 2007, capital markets assigned an approximately 20 bps risk differential between covered and senior unsecured bonds, as banks were perceived as very robust and low risk investments (Figure 3). This in turn resulted in a large value assigned to the residual claim of senior unsecured bank bonds. For the following year, as the GFC set in, these increased up to approximately 60 bps, (Dierks & Somerville, 2012) and jumped up to above 200 bps when tensions in the banking sector reached their height. After this nine month period, the spread dropped again to approximately 50 bps and remained steady since then.

Depending on economic and regulatory conditions, banks' preferences for different funding sources vary. Notably, during the 2000s, commercial banks exhibited a tendency to put stronger emphasis on interbank and money market funding, while putting less emphasis on deposit funding. However, as these markets were adversely affected during the GFC, their preference shifted towards collateralized funding sources (Caruana & van Rixtel, 2012).

---

[16] As all loans remain in the cover pool, which the issuer is obliged to maintain, the issuer bears all credit risk in a going concern scenario.

[17] Affinito and Tagliaferri (2010), Farruggio and Uhde (2015), and Martin-Oliver and Saurina (2007) also identify liquidity considerations to be the main driver for securitization.

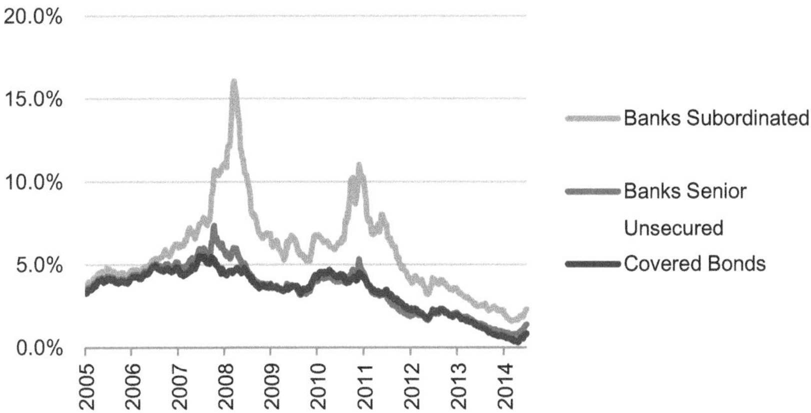

Figure 3: Yield Development of Bank Funding Instruments
Year marks represent the year end. All constituents are represented by yields of euro-denominated Markit iBoxxindexes Maturities are not matched. Source: Markit iBoxx

Covered bond emission volumes varied largely throughout the GFC. This is particularly true for the volumes emitted by periphery countries, which increased during the crisis until 2013 and thereby allowed for a stable funding basis of periphery banking sectors (Figure 4).

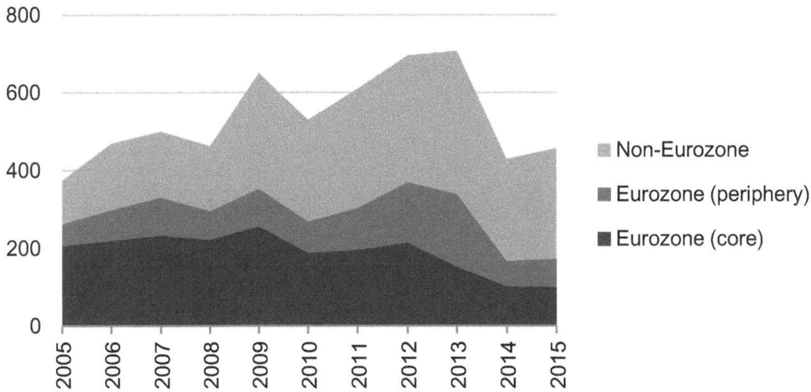

Figure 4: Covered Bond Emission Volume by Region
Covered emission bond volume is depicted in euro-billion. The periphery eurozone comprises of Cyprus, Greece, Ireland, Italy, Portugal, and Spain. Source: ECBC (2016)

2.2.3 *Regulatory Considerations*

Under the regulatory framework currently in place, covered bonds enjoy a preferential treatment,[18] making them an attractive funding instrument. Banks may access two different paths in utilizing their covered bonds to obtain funding.

First, they may deposit any covered bond in their possession as collateral with the ECB if it fulfills the collateral requirements (Will, 2009). However, under such repo-transactions, covered bonds are subject to a 15% haircut under high quality liquid assets (HQLA) requirements and therefore also towards the fulfillment of the requirements under the LCR.[19] Technically, a bank may obtain possession of covered bonds either via a purchase in the market, or by issuing the product backed by its own cover pool and retaining it on its own balance sheet, that is not selling it to external investors (Will, 2009). Self-issued covered bonds may therefore increase bank's liquidity position.

The second avenue, which has opened with the implementation of CBPP3, is to first retain covered bond issues on the banks balance sheet in order to sell them solely to the Eurosystem without any haircuts (Eichert, 2014).[20] In either case, they qualify as long-term funding under the NSFR, however, the retained portion counts towards long-term uses.

2.3 Investor Demand

Typical investors in covered bonds are banks, insurance companies, pension funds, and with a growing importance central banks. They value the low risk profile and deep liquidity of the market, which is only matched by the market for sovereign bonds.

2.3.1 *Risk Profile*

As previously mentioned, the risk profile of a covered bond changes upon the insolvency of the issuer. As such, investors are exposed to a changing set of risk factors (Table 4). If the issuer is going concern, the investor mostly faces the risk

---

[18] See Quirk (2010), and Stöcker (2014) for details on the regulatory treatment of covered bonds.

[19] According to the Bank of International Settlements (2013): "The objective of the LCR is to promote the short-term resilience of the liquidity risk profile of banks. It does this by ensuring that banks have an adequate stock of unencumbered HQLA that can be converted easily and immediately in private markets into cash to meet their liquidity needs for a 30 calendar day liquidity stress scenario."

[20] Note the 70% investment limit imposed under CBPP3. For details, refer to Table 10.

of the issuer's insolvency and therefore an inferior risk position. Only in the case of an issuer insolvency, the investor also gets exposed to cover pool risks, the risk of timely repayment, as well as structural and legal risk in connection with the immediate management of the cover pool.

Table 4: Investor Risks depending on Insolvency Status

	Pre Issuer Involvency	Post Issuer Insolvency
Issuer Risk	Yes	No
Cover Pool Risk	No	Yes
Risk of Timely Repayment	No	Yes
Structural and Legal Risks	No	Yes
Other Risks	Yes	Yes

Source: Spangler and Werner (2014)

Table 5 lists the detailed risks for German Pfandbrief investments. Particularly interesting is the fact, that upon insolvency of the issuer, the cover pool assets become fixed, much as in an MBS. Thereby, the investment becomes exposed to early redemption and extension risks.

Table 5: Detailed Investor Risks for German Pfandbrief Investments

Issuer Risk	Cover Pool Risk	Risk of Timely Repayment	Structural and Legal Risks	Other Risks
▪ Issuer Default Risk ▪ Cover Pool Management Risk ▪ Further CB Issuance ▪ Other Issuer related Risk	▪ Credit Risk ▪ Interest Rate Risk ▪ Currency Risk ▪ Refinancing Risk ▪ Reinvestment Risk ▪ Prepayment Risk ▪ Real Estate Risk	▪ Early Redemption Risk ▪ Extension Risk	▪ Country Risks ▪ Operational Risks ▪ Settlement Risk ▪ Settlement and Related Risks ▪ Reputational Risk ▪ Regulatory Risk	▪ Segregation Risk ▪ Transition to alternative Management ▪ Cover Pool Liquidation Risk

Source: Spangler and Werner (2014)

2.3.2 *Return Considerations*

Due to the low risk return profile, covered bonds are typically considered a complimentary to sovereign bonds in investment portfolios and are therefore subject to rebalancing effects between these two markets. Additionally, the heterogeneous covered bond markets allow for profitable rebalancing among different covered bond legislatures. The same holds true for standard trades taking advantage of different maturities, coupon structures, and liquidity.

If capital markets receive exogenous information leading to changes in the risk profile of different covered bonds, they adjust their portfolio weights to reflect these changes and maximize profit. As such, upon new information, which assumes a relative outperformance of low-quality covered bonds, investors tend to re-balance their portfolios towards these, leading to a decreasing yield of the low quality bonds due to larger demand, and possibly to a increasing yield of high quality bonds due to lower demand. At least, the gap between the two should become narrower.

The separation in high and low quality bonds generally depends on the information content of the news. Separations might take the form of countries (e.g., core vs. periphery), maturity, or issuer. The opposite reaction takes place, if the new information signals larger risks, leading investors to safeguard their investments by means of investing in high quality assets. This mechanism is broadly referred to as the market being in 'risk-on' and 'risk-off' mode, respectively.

The origin of the information changing investor expectations may come from a large array of sources. While information on the covered bond market, such as new issues, rating changes, or issuer financial reporting are among the most common ones, they might also be based in the areas of macroeconomics, monetary policy, and sovereign bond markets.

2.3.3 *Investor Groups*

With close to 40% of all emission volumes, banks represent the largest investor group in covered bonds (Figure 5). They are followed by asset management firms, pension funds and Insurances, as well as central banks. Banks tend to invest in covered bonds as means of asset liability management, their investment portfolio, and liquidity management. The intention of asset managers, pension funds and insurance companies on the other hand is to invest in an alternative to sovereign bonds with only a slightly more aggressive risk profile but also slightly larger return, while reaching long-term investment goals. The role of central banks is considered in more detail during the course of this investigation.[21]

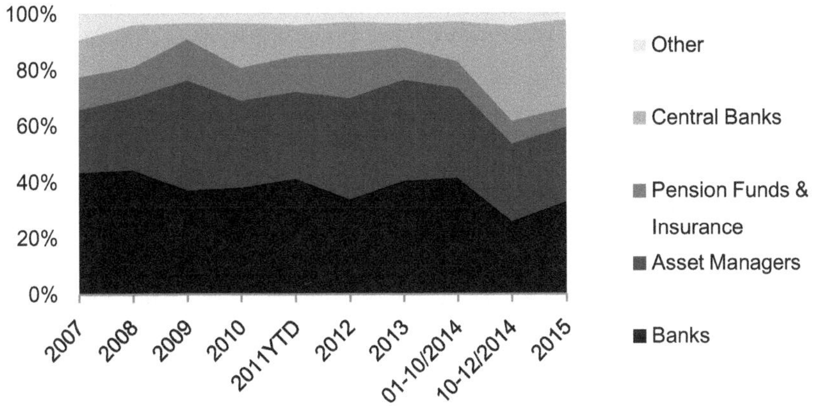

Figure 5: Benchmark Covered Bond Investors by Sector
2011YTD figure refers to the partial year until publication of the article and the split of 2014 represents the beginning of CBPP3. Source: Burmeister, Grossmann, and Stöcker (2011), Costa (2016)

2.3.4 *Regulatory Considerations*

Investments in covered bonds have several advantages from a regulatory point of view. Common to all investors is the fact that they are not subject to so called bail-in clauses, introduced in 2014.[22] This is due to the fact that the claim is secured by the cover pool, aiming to satisfy investor claims in the case of insolvency.

Asset managers and pension funds typically have self-imposed investment restrictions depending on rating, volume, geography and volatility. There is therefore no regulatory restriction for their investment in covered bonds, unless

[21] The approximately 5% investment of central banks in pre-crisis periods also includes supranational agencies and institutions close to central banks.

[22] As part of the EU Bank Recovery and Resolution Directive (2014/59), regulators are able to write banks liabilities down or convert them into equity, if a bank is endangered of becoming insolvent.

they are collective investment funds regulated under the Undertakings for Collective Investments in Transferable Securities (UCITS) directive.[23]

Covered bonds enjoy a preferential treatment under UCITS, due to the high credit quality of the instrument. This takes the form of an increased investment limit per issuer (typically 15 instead of 3% of all fund assets), and a larger prudential investment limit (25 instead of 5%, Price Waterhouse Coopers, 2012). Investors may therefore hold larger shares of covered bonds than of other assets.

Insurance companies on the other hand are to oblige the regulations set out in Solvency II. This framework requires capital requirements for certain AAA-rated bonds of only two thirds of that for lower rated covered bonds and AAA-rated senior unsecured and corporate bonds (Price Waterhouse Coopers, 2012).

As an investor in covered bonds, banks have to consider two regulatory measures under Basel III. First, they count towards the LCR, as previously mentioned with a 15% haircut under HQLA. This is preferential to ABS, which are subject to a larger haircut. Secondly, the NSFR requires banks to provide long-term funding for 20% of all covered bonds on their balance sheet rated AA- and above and 50% if rated between A+ and A-. The latter value is equivalent to loans to non-financial corporate and less than for residential mortgages with 65% (Price Waterhouse Coopers, 2012)

2.4 Market Structure and Pricing

Building on corporate bonds, the functionality of the covered bond market is largely the same. However, due to the differences in its legal design, a number of differences have been observed. This holds particularly true for credit risk considerations, while liquidity risk is largely in line with prevalent corporate bond literature.

2.4.1 Yield Development

Until 2008Q3, covered bonds traded in a very narrow band between the first and third quartile (Figure 6). With the collapse of Lehman Brothers, capital markets re-evaluated banking credit risk and the market widened substantially. This only

---

[23] UCITS is a European directive harmonizing the legal framework for collective investments in Europe and thereby allowing unrestricted operations and marketing within the European Union. Refer to directive 2009/65/EC of the European Parliament and of the Council as of July 13, 2013 for legal details.

reversed in the 2013Q4 and the covered bond sector most recently traded at a range similar to the pre-Lehman period.

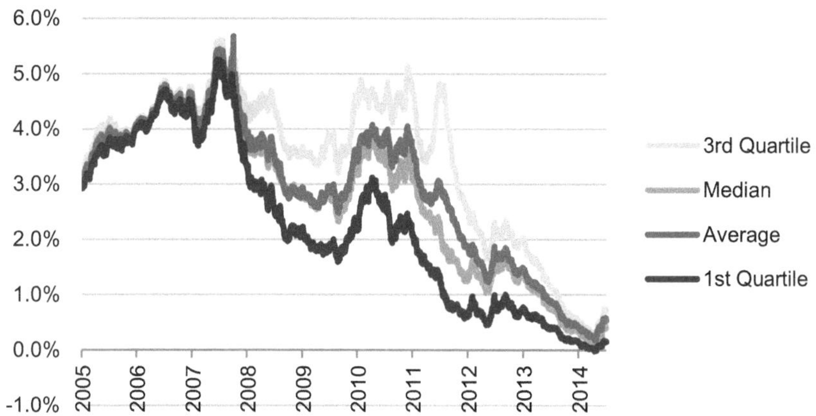

Figure 6: Quartile Covered Bond Yields

Quartile and average yields of covered bonds included in Markit iBoxx euro-denominated covered bond index. Year marks represent the year end. Source: Own illustration based on Datastream

During the period of 2005 to 2015, the covered bond yield level has changed substantially from approximately 3% in July 2005, via 5% in April 2008, to 0.5% in May 2015. However, the absolute level of covered bond yields reflects the interest rate level prevalent at each point in time, which has followed a similar development.

In order to avoid misinterpretation[24] in that regards, covered bonds are typically quoted in terms of yield spreads. The benchmark employed by sell-side institutions is the asset swap curve, while the buy-side also frequently also employs sovereign bond yields. The major difference between the two is the reflection of credit risk.

---

[24] That is mistakenly interpreting changes in the interest term structure as changes in credit and liquidity risk premia.

2.4.2 *Credit Risk*

The major difference between the two benchmarks is credit risk. The asset swap depicts the long-term money market rate in the interbank sector. As such, the interbank counterparty risk is included, as opposed to the overnight index swap. Using the sovereign bond rate, the sovereign default risk is already reflected.[25] Figure 7 depicts the credit risk for five year German sovereign bonds (Bunds) to be consistently lower than the interbank credit risk reflected in asset swaps. In turn, German covered bonds trade only slightly wider than the swap rate. As a reference, the combined index for all euro-denominated benchmark covered bonds traded substantially wider than that of Germany, partly reflecting additional sovereign risks.

Figure 7: Covered Bond Yields in Comparison to Benchmarks
Year marks represent the year end. Source: Own illustration based on Datastream and Markit iBoxx

It can also be noted that credit risk played a negligible role before the onset of the GFC, as for example has been confirmed by Breger and Stovel (2004) who find that individual bond ratings do not have a significant impact on covered bond pricing as the probability of default is marginal.

---

[25] Rating agencies use the sovereign rating as a ceiling to individual covered bond ratings and therefore assume the sovereign risk to be imminent in covered bonds.

Nonetheless, numerous studies find a risk premium of German mortgage covered bonds over German public covered bonds to be present (Schäfer & Hochstein, 1999; Birkmeyer & Herbert 2002; Breger & Stovel, 2004).[26] According to Volk and Hillenbrand (2006), part of covered bond risk premia can be attributed to different nationalities of the issuer. On the other hand this has been challenged by Packer et al. (2007) who only find a weak influence of the country of residence. Prokopczuk and Vonhoff (2012) were able to demonstrate that the quality of the cover pool has an impact on a covered bond's pricing in crisis times.

2.4.3 Liquidity

As previously noted, credit risk became a concern in covered bond pricing only since the onset of the GFC. Before, all differences in covered bond pricing have been perceived as differences in liquidity, which also remained a factor thereafter. In fact, considering bid-ask-spreads as a liquidity measure,[27] we note a very small liquidity premium until mid-2007 (Figure 8). During the 2008 to 2012 period, liquidity premiums remained high and have only decreased since 2012 and not reached pre-crisis levels again.

Contrary to the EBA,[28] Perraudin (2014) argues that bid-ask-spreads provide a good measure for liquidity in covered bond markets. He shows covered bonds and ABS exhibit comparable liquidity positions and some ABS have proven more liquid than covered bonds during the 2011 crisis.

Dick-Nielsen, Gyntelberg, and Sangill (2012) employ an idiosyncratic risk measure as proposed by Acharya and Pedersen (2005). In their study on high frequency trading impacts on Danish covered bonds, they find Danish covered bonds to have exhibited even greater liquidity during the 2008 crisis than Danish sovereign bonds. While the liquidity premia decreased in both markets thereafter, long-term covered bonds form an exception as liquidity risk remained larger than it was before the GFC. In their similar analysis also on the Danish market, Buchholst, Gyntelberg, and Sangill (2010) arrive at comparable results.

---

[26] The only difference between these two is the default probability of mortgage banks in the first case, versus that of the government and municipalities in the latter.

[27] For a discussion of alternative liquidity measures, see Chordia et al. (2005), and Hibbert, Kirchner, Kretzschmar, Li, and McNeil (2009)

[28] EBA abstains from using bid-ask-spreads for their analysis and classification of numerous asset classes for their HQLA classifications, due to data availability.

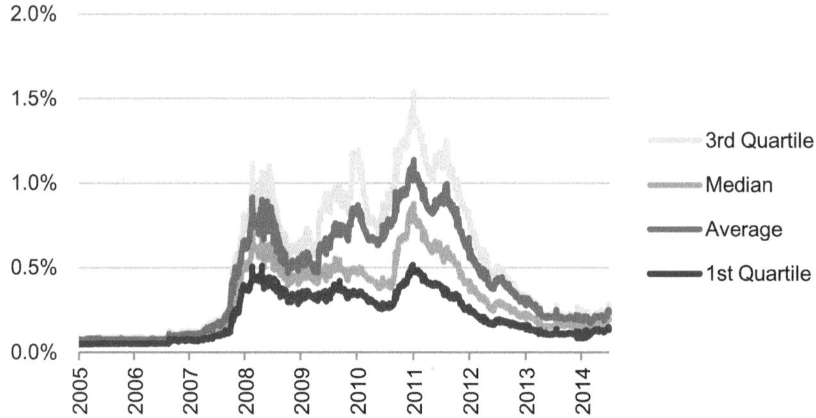

Figure 8: Quartile Covered Bond Bid-Ask-Spread

Quartile and average bid-ask-spreads of covered bonds included in Markit iBoxx euro-denominated covered bond index. The bid-ask-spread is defined as the proportional difference between the bid price and the ask price in relation to the ask price. Year marks represent the year end. Source: Own Illustration based on Datastream

More generally, Ericsson and Renault (2006) find the term structure of bonds and thereby the illiquidity term structure to be depending on the remaining time to maturity. The longer the remaining time to maturity, the lower the liquidity risk premium becomes. Such a differentiation of liquidity premia along the maturity axis are confirmed by further studies, such as Kempf, Korn, and Uhrig-Homburg's (2012)[29] analysis of the German sovereign and covered bond market, which is similar to Koziol and Sauerbier (2007). They find the short term and long term liquidity premia to be uncorrelated. While the first is captured by capital market volatility, the latter is driven by long-term economic outlook.

[29] Kempf et al. (2012) and Koziol and Sauerbier (2007) argue, that German sovereign bonds and German benchmark covered bonds exhibit negligible credit risk and the spread difference is therefore attributable to liquidity risk only.

3 Unconventional Monetary Policy

Unconventional monetary policy is an umbrella term for policy instruments, which a central bank would only use when its traditional tool-box is either exhausted or has lost its effectiveness in meeting the challenges it faces. This is generally the case, when the conventional tool of short-term interest setting reaches its limits at its natural lower bound at zero. During the GFC, central banks have largely resorted to outright asset purchases of sovereign and corporate bonds, which include covered bonds.[30]

For the purpose of this analysis, we focus on unconventional monetary measures that impact banks ability to obtain sufficient and attractively priced funding. Further, we focus on programs in markets with sizable covered bond volumes outstanding.

3.1 Background

In December 2008, the Federal Reserve set its central bank interest rate to 0.25% and the Bank of England to 0.5% in March 2009. The ECB followed with a rate of 1.0% in May 2009. These three central banks were therefore approaching the lower zero bound. While central banks' ability to further influence markets in this situation was disputed for a long time, Fawley and Neely (2013), for example, argue that this was not the case. In such cases, central banks would be able to increase liquidity and the monetary base, leading to inflationary pressure and economic stimulation, particularly when taking the form of long-term asset purchases (e.g., Mishkin, 1996; Bernanke, 2002). However, Gern, Jansen, Kooths, and Wolters (2015) find ambiguous empirical results in their review of the prevalent literature. If the liquidity employed in asset purchases is not withdrawn from the financial system elsewhere,[31] this is referred to as quantitative easing.

Pattipeilohy, van den End, Tabbae, Frost, and de Haan (2013, p. 118) identify three elements of unconventional monetary policy frameworks:

---

[30] Refer to Pattipeilohy et al. (2013) for an overview of conventional and unconventional monetary policy in the eurozone.

[31] A monetary policy measure is called sterilized if the net monetary base does not change, that is, liquidity is reduced in the same amount in a different segment for each additional instrument.

H. Markmann, *Covered Bonds under Unconventional Monetary Policy*,
Essays in Real Estate Research 14,
https://doi.org/10.1007/978-3-658-20975-9_3

> "(i) large-scale liquidity support to banks; (ii) forward guidance of ultra-low policy rates over extended policy horizons; and (iii) large-scale financial market interventions, in particular huge asset purchases."

According to Gern et al. (2015), QE measures are most effective when capital markets are in distress and the central bank interest rate has not yet reached its zero lower bound. Bluwstein and Canova (2016) even conclude that unconventional monetary policy announcement lead to financial market responses, which are similar to conventional monetary shocks, if they arrive at surprise.

The bank of Japan was the first central bank to approach the zero lower bound in 2001, when it abandoned the overnight interest rate as its main policy tool, and instead instated the amount of central bank balances as its main monetary policy measure. During the course of 2001 to 2006, their goal increased from ¥4 to 35 trillion, which it aimed to reach via sovereign and private sector bond purchases. However, the program ended unsuccessfully in 2006 with reinstating of the overnight interest rate as a policy target (Fawley & Neely, 2013).

In the aftermath of the Lehman Brothers insolvency and the during the GFC, the Bank of England, Bank of England, Federal Reserve, and ECB conducted unconventional monetary policy interventions, which next to others, took the shape of forward looking policy statements, liquidity injections and outright bond purchases.[32]

3.2 Unconventional Monetary Policy in the Eurozone

Triggered by the US subprime crisis and the insolvency of Lehman Brothers, the eurozone has been subject to continuous crises, which are characterized by deficiencies in different areas of capital markets. The first one directly arose from Lehman Brothers' insolvency and resulted in a large degree of uncertainty in the banking sector. The second one extended to the fear of sovereign states failing and is called the sovereign debt crisis. The third phase on the other hand, mostly silently involves a muted continuation of the sovereign debt crisis but is most importantly driven by deflationary tendencies and the ECB's inability to employ traditional monetary policy measures.

---

32 For an extensive overview of the unconventional monetary policy measures of all four central banks and the respective market conditions, reter to Fawley and Neely (2013). Further summaries are provided by Lenza et al. (2010), Hamilton and Wu, (2012) and Cour-Thiemann and Winkler (2013).

3.2.1 Global Financial Crisis and Banking Crisis

The US subprime crisis was triggered by a burst of the local housing bubble and led to losses for a large number of investors of MBS. In addition to Bear Stearns being taken over by J.P. Morgan, Lehman Brothers filed for Chapter 11 bankruptcy protection on the back of accruing losses in the subprime mortgage sector in September 2008. Along with this process, it became evident that subprime losses were a systemic risk for the US banking sector. As the exact amount of subprime losses to any bank were largely unknown, the uncertainty among banks and counterparty risk premia rose. Due to the close connection of the international banking sector, these tensions also extended to Europe.

Counterparty risk in the banking sector is generally demonstrated via the spread between the local Libor and Overnight Indexed Swap (OIS) rate. The difference between the two is that the libor rate constitutes an unsecured interbank lending rate and is therefore subject to counterparty risk, while the OIS is considered a risk free central bank rate. Figure 9 depicts the 6M Euribor versus the 6M EONIA rate. While the tensions became evident in the fall of 2007, when the subprime crisis became emerged, counterparty risk spiked after the Lehman Brothers bankruptcy and only eased in the beginning of 2009.

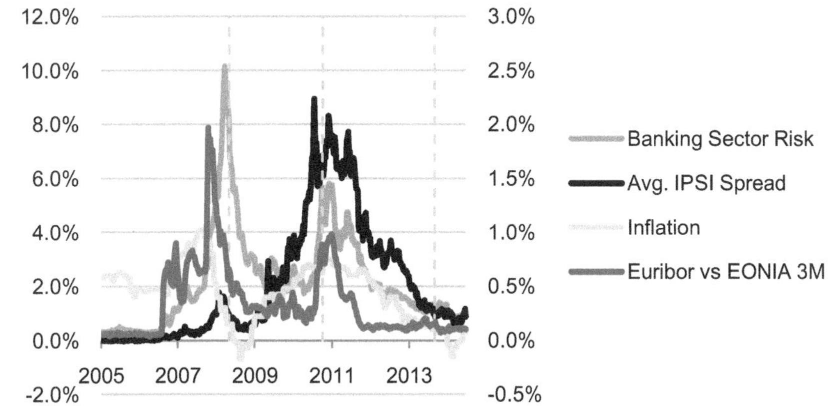

Figure 9: Development of Bank Risk Measures

Euribor vs. EONIA 3M on secondary axis. Verticals lines represent CBPP announcements. Source: Datastream

At this time, the Bank of England and the Federal Reserve dramatically cut their central bank interest rates (as above mentioned) and implemented large scale asset purchase programs.[33] The ECB on the other hand, opted for a different set of measures:

In September 2008, the ECB announced a "special term refinancing operation [...] to improve the overall liquidity position of the euro area banking system" (ECB, 2008), which would be unlimited in volume and have a maturity of one month. As the counterparty risk continued to rise, the same procedure was formalized in a program called fixed-rate tender, full allotment (FRFA), which was announced in October 2008. While the ECB previously auctioned refinancing tenders at two weeks, called main refinancing operations (MRO), and at three months, called longer-term refinancing operations (LTRO) at fixed quantities, now the rate was fixed, while providing unlimited liquidity. However, banks could only access these facilities when able to pledge sufficient collateral. To avoid a shortage of the latter, the eligibility criteria were eased (Fawley & Neely, 2013).[34]

In addition to lowering the central bank interest rate, the Federal Reserve announced outright purchases of treasuries, government sponsored enterprises,[35] and MBS in the amount of $1.8 trillion until May 2009 (Gagnon, Raskin, Remacht, & Sack, 2011). To a lower extend, the Bank of England announced outright purchases of private assets and British government bonds (Gilts) in an amount of £175 billion (Joyce, Lasaosa, Stevens, & Tong, 2011).

By May 2009, the funding landscape for European banks had gone through several stages. While it had practically shut down in the immediate aftermath of the Lehman Brothers bankruptcy, few issuers entered the jumbo covered bond market in January 2009. However, this came at the price of greater spreads compared to the pre-Lehman period (Figure 15). Until March, credit spreads continued to rise and the market discriminated much stronger for credit risk, as can be seen from the larger yield differences for several European covered bond indexes (Figure 10; Burmeister, 2009). The market generally exhibited a large degree of uncertainty with regards to further bank failures.

---

[33] For details on the Federal Reserve's program, refer to Section 3.3.2.

[34] For details on the easing of credit quality requirements, refer to Gabor (2012), and Koulischer and Struyven (2014).

[35] That is, the three mortgage institutions Fannie Mae, Freddie Mac, and Ginnie Mae

In order to mitigate this fragility in the banking sector, the ECB and numerous sovereign governments implemented countermeasures. In May 2009, the ECB announced a set of three twelve-month LTRO facilities (June to December 2009), as well as its first outright bond purchase program. Under the latter, the Eurosystem was to acquire covered bonds in a total amount of €60 billion in the primary and secondary market over a one-year period.[36] Its aim was to strengthen the covered bond market by tightening secondary market spreads and to support emission activity, in order to avoid funding difficulties (Table 6; Appendix 1). CBPP1 is anecdotally reported to have led to an increased emission activity in the covered bond market upon the mere announcement of the program (Burmeister, 2009; Winkler, 2009).

Table 6: Eurosystem's Covered Bond Purchase Programs in Perspective

	CBPP1	CBPP2	CBPP3
Characteristics			
Volume	€60 bn	€40 bn	< €10 bn monthly
Duration	12M	12M	Initially 24M
Key Risk Measures at Announcement			
Euribor vs EONIA 3M	0.6%	0.7%	0.2%
Avg. IPSI vs. Bunds	0.7%	6.1%	0.9%
Eurozone Inflation	0.6%	3.0%	0.4%
Economic Rationale			
Crisis Type	Banking Crisis	Sovereign Debt Crisis	Deflationary Tendency
Source	Easing Bank Funding	Banking Sector Liquidification	Expansion of Monetary Base
Additional Program	12M LTRO		ABSPP

Source: Own illustration

In addition to the ECB, numerous sovereign government introduced government guarantees for certain bank bonds. These were introduced on a country level and therefore been tailored to the banking system and condition at the

36 See Sections 5.1 and 6.1 for program details and previous research on the Eurosystem's CBPPs.

time.[37] Further, the numerous bank bail-outs present an unusual form of liquidity injection into the banking sector.

3.2.2 Sovereign Debt Crisis

The European sovereign debt crisis first became evident when the Greek government corrected its budget deficit for 2009 to 12.9% of GDP in October 2009 and applied for emergency funding with the International Monetary Fund (IMF) in April 2010. While Greece provides the first and most drastic case, numerous European countries have experienced difficulties in funding their budgets and debt obligations. Most notable are Greece, Ireland, and Portugal. Their struggles were caused by a number of interlinked factors, which include structural budgetary deficits, non-structural deficits for buffering the effects of the economic downturn of the GFC, productivity disadvantages, bursts of housing bubbles, and the inability to devalue the national currency due to eurozone membership.

These events led the ECB to announce its SMP in order to acquire sovereign debt from Greece, Ireland, and Portugal in the open market in May 2010. The SMP aimed at providing a support to weak demand for such periphery sovereign bonds, and ease their ability to attract capital market finance.

At the same time, the governments of the eurozone countries, the ECB, and the IMF continued to work on emergency funding and packages for those countries most severely affected. These measures included maturity extensions, a reduction of the interest on outstanding debt, and the implementation of the European Financial Stability Facility (EFSF), which had mandate to provide emergency loans to sovereigns, intervene in primary and secondary debt markets, conduct precautionary programs, and to finance the recapitalization of financial institutions by means of loans to sovereigns. The ECB member states capitalized the facility with guarantees in the amount of €780 billion, allowing lending in the volume of €440 billion.

With a continued weak development of the economy, the burst of the Spanish housing bubble and an increasing indebtedness of Italy, the sovereign debt crisis continued to spread to Cyprus, Italy, and Spain during the course of 2011 and then also affected large countries. The level of the average five year sover-

[37] For an overview of the European government guaranteed bonds, refer to Grande, Levy, Panetta, and Zaghini (2011) and Levy and Schich (2010).

eign yield for Italy, Portugal, Spain, and Ireland (Figure 9) reached up to 8% larger versus Bunds in 2010 and 2011.

This led the ECB to announce the reactivation of the SMP with the purpose of acquiring Italian and Spanish sovereign bonds in the secondary market in August 2011. As per December 2012, the Eurosystem held sovereign bonds in a total amount of €218 billion. Of these, €14.2 billion were from Ireland, and €33.9, 44.3, 402.8, and 22.8 billion from Greece, Spain, Italy, and Portugal, respectively (ECB, 2013).

As the eurozone governments, the ECB, and the IMF were not able to find a sufficient solution to the imminent default of either of those countries, spreads remained at similar levels until the fall of 2012.

In addition to the difficulties based in the bursting of housing bubbles, the sovereign debt crisis impacted the banking sector through several channels. First, banks are a large investor group in sovereign bonds, particularly of the respective own country. A default of a sovereign would therefore have led to an immediate write-off of a large amount of bank assets. Second, rating agencies generally apply a rating ceiling at the same level of the sovereign, and capital markets consider government risk as part of a bond's credit risk. Third, the larger the credit risk of a sovereign, the less worthy are guarantees issued by that very sovereign and the lower is its ability to bail out a failing bank. Finally, the larger a country's debt burden, the lower is its ability to stimulate economic growth. Therefore, all debt instruments of banks in these countries affected were subject to a lower rating and thereby to higher funding costs, as well as a depressed outlook. As expected, the eurozone Libor-OIS spread confirms this by reaching a height at the end of 2011 (Figure 9).

These effects in turn led to a substantial slowing of the covered bond market in the summer of 2011. However, market participants did not consider it shut, but instead recognize a shift towards smaller issues. Nonetheless, the difficulty to obtain covered bond funding at the rates prevailing for periphery countries was apparent (Figure 10). However, the slower covered bond market was only perceived secondary to the difficulty in obtaining unsecured funding.

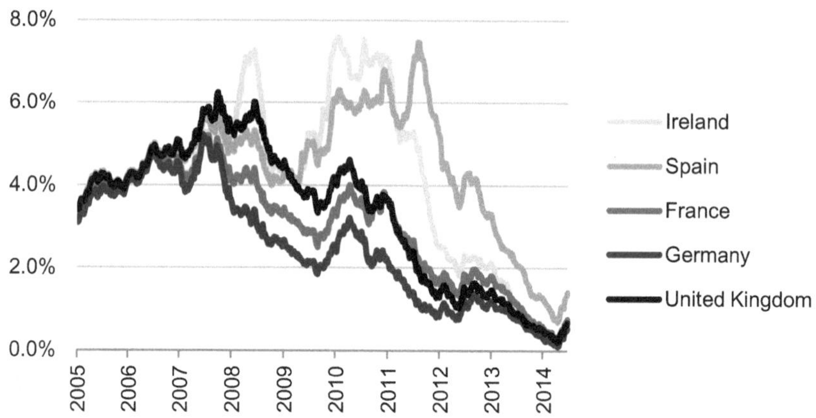

Figure 10: iBoxx Covered Bond Yields
Year marks represent the year end. Source: Datastream, Markit

In August 2011, the ECB announced a second CBPP, expected to acquire covered bonds in an amount of €40 billion in primary and secondary markets over a one year time span. However, the program suffered from three deficiencies:

To mitigate the continued difficulty in banks attaining sufficient funding, the ECB announced two twelve-month LTRO operations in October 2011, and expanded the December LTRO facility to 36 months for December and February 2012. The latter is referred to as LTRO2 and provided banks with a total liquidity of €842.5 billion. In the time span between September 2011 and January 2012, the ECB had increased the monetary base by 50% (Gern et al., 2015). Szczerbowicz (2015) finds the announcement of the LTRO2 to have led to a 22-bp reduction of the Libor-OIS spread.

When the sovereign debt crisis was still not resolved and the sovereign yields for periphery countries remained at high levels, and the idea of a break-up of the eurozone started to float, the ECB president Mario Draghi held its "Whatever it takes"-speech at a London conference. The key quote is as follows: "Within our mandate, the ECB is ready to do whatever it takes to preserve the euro. And believe me, it will be enough." (Draghi, 2012) Following this first indication, the ECB indicated an outright sovereign bond purchase program at its August governing council meeting. The OMT program was announced in September and entails the purchase of sovereign debt in secondary markets order to provide an emergency liquidity facility to ensure the liquidity position of eurozone sovereigns. The OMT replaced the SMP.

The OMT however is rather restrictive in its regulation. Purchases are conditional to the member country being granted aid from the EFSF / European Stability Mechanism (ESM), which was still to be established as of that date, and to having regained access to capital markets. Additionally, purchases may only take place on a sterilized basis.

The above mentioned ESM is the successor to the EFSF and has a total lending capacity of €500 billion.[38] Its aim is to provide emergency financial aid to member countries, which are in financial difficulty. Its funds may also be employed for bank recapitalization, as a €100 billion recapitalization of the Spanish banking sector, for which the sovereign applied in July 2012 (ESM, 2017).

Only after these events, capital markets gained confidence in periphery sovereigns and their yields started to reflect the lower credit risk.

3.2.3 Deflationary Pressure and Fragile Growth

The subsequent two years were characterized by continued low interest rates and low inflation (Figure 9), as well as a weak economic development in the whole eurozone but particularly in core countries. Partly driven by austerity measures, partly driven by the unwillingness for economic reforms, a number of periphery countries experienced a very low economic growth, partly even recessions. Additionally, inflation expectations in late 2014 and early 2015 began to indicate deflationary tendencies, leading the ECB to look for measures to revert the inflation rate towards its target and to avoid a deflation (Constâncio, 2015; Dunne, Everett, & Stuart, 2015).

In fact, Gern et al. (2015) observe a decrease in the monetary base in 2013/14, which implicitly results in a monetary policy tightening, without explicitly being announced. Building on these principles of unconventional monetary policy, however, the ECB began again to expand the monetary base in order to attain a higher inflation rate.

[38] In addition to the ESFM, the ESM also replaces the European Financial Stability Mechanism (EFSM), which serves a similar purpose but is guaranteed by the European Commission.

As a first measure, the ECB announced its Targeted Longer-Term Refinancing Operation (TLTRO) in June 2014. Its implementation came before the maturity of LTRO2 in December, which would have led to a substantial reduction of liquidity in the banking system and therefore potentially harmed lending to the real economy. Under TLTRO, banks were given the opportunity to borrow an amount relative to its lending. TLRO lending would take place until June 2016 and mature in September 2014 (ECB, 2014)

Surprising capital markets, the ECB also announced a third CBPP in combination with an Asset Backed Securities Purchase Programme (ABSPP) in September 2014. While its volume was initially not announced, the combined volume was later specified to €10 billion per month. At the time of the announcement, market participants recognized that there was no need for a covered bond purchase program from a bank funding perspective, as the counterparty risk measure was very low (Figure 9) and covered bond spreads were mostly trading as tightly as in pre-crisis levels (Figure 10).

Along the same lines of argumentation, the ECB announced its Public Sector Purchase Program (PSPP) in January 2015, which was to acquire sovereign debt. In combination with CBPP3 and the ABSPP, these were called Extended Asset Purchase Programme (EAPP) and scheduled bonds in an amount of €60 billion per month, at least until September 2016 (ECB 2014, Dunne et al., 2015). This results in a total purchase volume of €1.2 trillion. Again, there was no obvious reason that would have called for tighter sovereign debt yields, and the program is expected to extend the monetary base.

3.3 Covered Bond Purchases in other Currency Areas

Except for the Eurosystem, only the Swiss National Bank has conducted outright purchases of covered bonds. However, the Federal Reserve conducted outright purchases of MBS as part of its LARP program.

3.3.1 Swiss National Bank's Covered Bond Purchase Program

In its March 2009 quarterly monetary policy assessment, the SNB announced a number of monetary policy announcement, such as a lower Libor target, interventions in the foreign exchange market, repo operations of a longer maturity, and the purchase of private sector issues. The latter was introduced in order to "bring about a relaxation of conditions on the capital markets", which was required, since "capital market risk premia have risen substantially since the collapse of Lehman Brother, hampering the transmission of monetary policy stimuli." (Swiss National Bank, 2009, p. 3)

The announcement did not specify the type or volume of the private sector bonds to be acquired. As such, capital markets had to educate themselves via the observation of the SNB's purchases. For the first three weeks of the program, these exclusively focused on covered bonds of the two Swiss covered bond issuers Pfandbriefbank and Pfandbriefzentrale (Kettemann & Krogstrup, 2014).

The majority of the CHF3 billion secondary market covered bond purchases was conducted in the first month of the program in March 2009. These ended in September and the program was abandoned in December of the same year. Taking into account the CHF64 billion Swiss covered bond market size, the SNB's purchases amounted to a total of approximately 5% of the covered bond market. Between March and August of 2010, the SNB disposed of its covered bond holdings without explicitly informing capital markets, which are assumed to have learned about the disposals after the fact (Kettemann & Krogstrup, 2014).

Kettemann and Krogstrup (2014) find a 10 basis point (bp) tightening of Swiss covered bond spreads versus sovereign bonds for the announcement of the program. On the other hand, the actual purchases and dispositions of covered bonds in the market did not lead to a change in covered bond spreads. Their results suggest covered bond markets to recognize and react very efficiently[39] to the announcement of outright covered bond purchases and not to be subject to portfolio rebalancing effects due to the actual purchases or sales in the open market, independently of the information available.

3.3.2 Federal Reserve's Large-Scale Asset Purchases 1

In November 2008, the Fed announced the acquisition of $100 billion in GSE debt and $500 billion in MBS, which was expanded by an additional $100 billion in GSE debt, $750 billion MBS, and $300 billion in March 2009 (Fawley & Neely, 2013). The combination of these two announcements is generally referred to as Large-Scale Asset Purchases (LSAP), or commonly Quantitative Easing 1 (QE1). The Federal Reserve had thereby decided to engage in quantitative easing at an early stage throughout the GFC and stated that the goal of its purchases was

[39] Covered bond purchases started immediately after the announcement at 2:00pm.

to "reduce the cost and increase the availability of credit for the purchase of houses, which in turn should support housing markets and foster improved conditions in financial markets more generally." (Federal Reserve, 2008) While the program did not engage in covered bond purchases, we review its effects on the basis of their proximity to covered bonds.

The majority of research on quantitative easing is concerned with the announcement effect on sovereign bonds. As such, Kilponen, Laakkonen, and Vilmunen (2015) find a large effects tightening effect, which is in line with Gagnon et al (2011), Hamilton and Wu (2012), and Krishnamurthy and Vissing-Jorgensen (2011).

When considering the rate effect on MBS, US researchers have mostly chosen to investigate the mortgage rate offered to new customers instead of the MBS rate. The only study considering respective announcement effects is Fuster and Willen (2010), who find mortgage rates to be 50 bps lower compared to the pre-LSAP announcement period.

On the other hand, a number of authors consider the actual implementation of the LSAP when determining its effect on the mortgage rate. For example, Krishnamurthy and Vissing-Jorgensen (2011) find QE1 to have led to lower MBS and corporate yields. However, they only arrive at this conclusion via recognizing decreased CDS costs for the respective bonds. Stroebel and Taylor (2009) only find a very small or insignificant impact of LSAP on the mortgage rate.

Finally, Hancock and Passmore (2011), find outright MBS and sovereign bond purchases to lead to a tightening of MBS yields. In fact, they find an in investment of the Fed in 24% of all outstanding MBS, equivalent to $1.21 billion, to have led to a 55 bps tighter yield. Similarly, a 22% investment of all sovereign bonds, equivalent to $1.93 trillion, led to a MBS yield tightening of 76 bps.

3.4 Transmission Mechanism

Numerous channels have been proposed and tested, through which unconventional monetary affects its desired outcome of inducing inflationary pressure and possibly to support economic growth. Additionally, covered bond purchases have a direct effect on the covered bond market.

3.4.1 Transmission Mechanism in General

There is no consistent framework for the transmission channels of unconventional monetary policy. However, most authors agree on a set of three to five channels. Gern et al. (2015) identify the signaling, portfolio (re-)balancing, and exchange rate channels. Neely (2015) does not identify the exchange rate channel, but instead elaborates on the liquidity channel. While Joyce et al. (2011) identify a subset of the above; Faliagarda and Reitz (2015) omit the foreign exchange rate channel, but introduce the bank lending channel. Further authors (e.g., Krishnamurthy & Vissing-Jorgensen, 2011; Krishnamurthy, Nagel, & Vissing-Jorgensen, 2014) identify additional transmission channels, such as the duration risk, prepayment risk, and default risk channels, which have not gained popularity. It is not always possible to clearly separate of these channels, as they result in the same goal.

Dunne et al. (2015) identify the three main channels of signaling, portfolio (re-) balancing and bank lending for asset purchase programs. The main rationale for their effectiveness is as follows:

The central bank decides to conduct an unsterilized outright assets purchase program and thereby to extend the monetary base. The purchases of long-term assets, which are mostly sovereign bonds, but are not limited to these, experience an increase in price and a drop in yield levels. The primary goal of outright asset purchase programs is therefore to ensure a consistently low sovereign interest rate throughout the term structure, but particularly on the long end. The key assumption is that the low long-term (sovereign) interest rate leads credit institutions to underwrite new loans at rates reflecting the lower term structure. If this is achieved, conventional monetary transmission mechanisms return into place: The low interest rate incentivizes consumption instead of saving, and entrepreneurs are encouraged to invest. With both stimulating the economy, a rising interest rate is expected (Figure 11; e.g., Mishkin, 1996; Dunne et al., 2015; Gern et al., 2015).

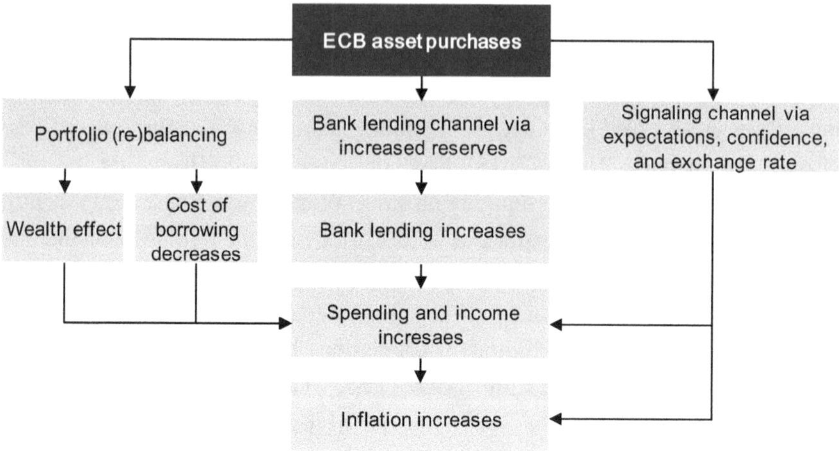

Figure 11: Transmission Channels of Asset Purchases to the Macro Economy
Liquidity premium and Foreign Exchange Rate channels were omitted. Source: Dunne et al. (2015)

The explicitly listed transmission channels provide further detail and are only described to the point, where conventional monetary policy transmission channels become effective.

3.4.1.1 Signaling Channel

The first channel is signaling, which entail all communication by the respective central bank, particularly with respect to its future actions. Such forward looking guidance leads market participants to adjust their expectations on the future development of the interest rate. The aim of interest rate signaling is to ensure an expectation of an extended low central bank interest rate, which would then translate into the term structure (Joyce et al., 2011; Faliagarda & Reitz, 2015). According to Gern et al. (2015), the announcement of additional unconventional monetary policy measures, such as outright asset purchases also channel through signaling in that they underline the severity of the economic condition and further lead to the expectation of a low interest rate. The signaling channel therefore aims at establishing the expectation for low short term rates.

While Gagnon et al. (2011) find the signaling channel to be the least important, Krishnamurthy and Vissing-Jorgensen (2011) find evidence for its effectiveness, and Bauer and Rudebusch (2013) claim the signaling channel to account for 35 to 65% of unconventional monetary policy effectiveness in lowering 10 year treasury yields.

3.4.1.2 Portfolio (Re-)Balancing Channel

The portfolio (re-)balancing channel is triggered via a central bank engaging in outright long term asset purchases. These purchases need to be sufficient in size to reduce the market supply of the asset, leading to an increase in price, and therefore a lower yield. Investors are likely to divest from this artificially less attractive asset class and instead invest in more risky asset classes (Faliagarda & Reitz, 2015).

This (re-)balancing may occur upon the mere announcement of an asset purchase program, or upon its implementation. It would lead to a lower yield of the long-term assets acquired by the central bank and therefore to a reduction in long-term interest rates (Joyce et al., 2011).

Numerous studies have found the portfolio (re-)balancing channel to be very important in analyzing unconventional monetary policy interventions (e.g., Gagnon et al., 2011; Joyce et al., 2011). The same holds true for Ketteman and Krogstrup (2013), who are able to preclude signaling channel effects and therefore fully attribute their findings to the (re-)balancing channel. Joyce et al (2011), explicitly confirm that the channel exerts its largest impact depressing medium and long-term sovereign bond yields. Eser and Schwab (2015) find evidence for the portfolio (re-)balancing channel in that they determine five-year sovereign bonds to trade 3 bps tighter for purchases in the amount of 1/1000 of the respective outstanding debt.

3.4.1.3 Liquidity Premium Channel

In normal times, capital markets are expected to be deep and liquid. However, when stressed, there might be a substantial uncertainty of execution and liquidity premia rise accordingly. If a central bank has engaged in an outright asset purchase program, it serves as a permanent and willing investor. It would additionally be inclined to accept a higher price under its portfolio (re-)balancing expectation. According to Christensen and Gillan (2016), the central bank thereby reduces downside the risk for investors. Additionally, they face lower selling costs, when inclined to do so and the market functioning improves (Faliagarda & Reitz, 2015). This effect, however, is temporarily limited to the duration of the outright asset purchase program (Joyce et al., 2011). The aim of the liquidity premium channel is therefore to improve market functionality.

For the Federal Reserve's Quantitative Easing Program 2 (QE2), Christensen and Gillan (2016) find a 10 to 13 bps lower liquidity premium between non-eligible treasury inflation protected securities (TIPS) and Treasury notes, which is in line with Gagnon et al. (2011).

3.4.1.4 Bank Lending Channel

The bank lending channel is based on an expansion of the monetary base, leading to a larger volume of central bank reserves for commercial banks. These on the other hand, may be employed for the banks credit business (Faliagarda & Reitz, 2015). The bank lending channel specifically refers to the volume of liquidity made available, as opposed to the rate (Creel, Hubert, & Viennot, 2013). The aim of the bank lending channel is therefore to increase the volume of bank lending to the real economy.

In their empirical analysis of the European banking landscape, Creel, Hubert, and Viennot (2013), however, find no evidence for the bank lending channel to support the bank lending volumes and even a negative effect with respect to the interest rate.

3.4.1.5 Foreign Exchange Rate Channel

Gern et al. (2015) build on the fact that an unsterilized expansion of the monetary base leads to a depreciation of the currency. This would in turn result in an increased export and economic activity. The aim of the foreign exchange rate channel is therefore to devalue the local currency, and improve economic activity. Gern et al.'s argument is confirmed by Diez and Presno (2014), who find a depreciation of the US-dollar upon the announcement of QE measures, as well as Neely (2015), who arrives at similar conclusions for the British Pound.

3.4.2 Transmission Mechanism of Covered Bond Purchases

The Eurosystem's CBPPs were not sterilized, they lead to an expansion of the monetary base and would therefore qualify under the above transmission mechanisms. The CBPPs are unlikely to lead to a direct signaling, however, would qualify under Gern et al.'s (2015) indication for the general shape of the monetary policy. The portfolio (re-)balancing and foreign exchange channels seem very viable, however, it has to be noted that CBPP1 and CBPP2 are relatively small (Watfe, 2015), compared to the effects found for the US economy by Hancock and Passmore (2011). While an economy-wide effect is therefore doubtable and has largely been neglected (Szczerbowicz, 2015; Watfe, 2015), the program might have led to intra-sector re-balancing effects and might have led to an effect via the bank lending channel. The liquidity channel seems also very likely to be effective for the covered bond market.

This assessment is based on the rationale for unconventional monetary policy with respect to mitigating deflationary tendencies and promoting economic growth. While this is the case for CBPP3, their applicability for CBPP1 and CBPP2 is to be doubted (Table 6).

Additionally, the above transmission mechanisms assume a homogeneous market of assets to be purchased, such as US treasury notes. However, European sovereign bonds and covered bonds are inherently heterogeneous, most obvious in credit risk. We therefore expect secondary intra-sector portfolio (re-)balancing effects. That is, Eurosystem purchases in the German covered bond market may either lead to a re-balancing into more risky asset classes, such as corporate bonds, or into more risky covered bonds, such as those of periphery countries.

The fact that the Eurosystem conducted outright covered bond purchases in the primary and secondary market, leads to several expected effects on covered bond yields. These are partially contrary to each other:

- Outright covered bond purchases in the secondary market lower covered bond yields.
- Lower covered bond yields as per the above lead to an increased emission activity, in turn increasing covered bond yields, as supply increases.[40]
- The Eurosystem placing orders in covered bond emissions lowers covered bond emission yields, as the demand for subscription increases.
- While the Eurosystem conducts outright covered bond purchases the liquidity increases, leading to a lower liquidity premium and covered bond yields decrease as per Section 6.

40 This assumption is tested in Section 4.

- After the Eurosystem has abandoned outright covered bond purchases, the liquidity decreases due to the lower market volume available and covered bond yields increase.[41]

[41] Assuming the ECB continues to hold purchases under the three CBPPs until maturity.

4 Impact on Emission Activity[42]

During the GFC, funding conditions for European banks deteriorated and led the ECB to initiate counter measures to improve banks' ability to provide credit to the real economy and to lower the interest term structure. Among the unconventional monetary policy measures introduced were the outright purchases of sovereign and covered bonds. The three CBPPs are unique, because, in addition to the secondary market, the Eurosystem acquired covered bonds in the primary market.[43]

The first CBPP was announced in May 2009, when banks experienced difficulties in capital market funding and the market for covered bond emissions nearly halted (Jobst, Kiff, & Spackman, 2009). Of the €60 billion covered bond purchases conducted under CBPP1, €16.2 billion (ECB, 2010) took place in the primary market and reportedly led to a broad re-opening of the market segment (Burmeister, 2009).[44] Driven by the sovereign debt crisis, the covered bond market slowed down but remained active in the fall of 2011, whereas the market for unsecured debt was largely dysfunctional. To provide sufficient liquidity to the banking sector, the ECB announced CBPP2 in October 2011. Scheduled at €40 billion, the program fell short at purchases of €16 billion, of which €6 billion were directed to the primary market (ECB, 2011). Before the implementation of CBPP3, on the other hand, covered bond markets were in sound order and the program was considered to serve an extension of the monetary base at approximately €10 billion per month. As of June 2015, 18% of these purchases took place in the primary market (ECB 2016).

The transmission channels of outright covered bond purchases affect primary and secondary markets. In the primary markets, the Eurosystem acting as anchor investor increases the probability of emitting covered bonds, and the initial yields decrease, because the investor demand for new issues is *ceteris paribus* larger. Thus far, the literature has focused on the CBPPs' effects on the

---

42 This Section is co-authored by Heidi Falkenbach.

43 Primary market purchases of sovereign debt are prohibited under Article 123 of the Treaty on the Functioning of the European Union.

44 At substantially larger spreads compared to pre-crisis levels.

H. Markmann, *Covered Bonds under Unconventional Monetary Policy*,
Essays in Real Estate Research 14,
https://doi.org/10.1007/978-3-658-20975-9_4

secondary market (Beirne et al. 2011; Szczerbowicz, 2015; Gibson et al., 2015), finding a slight decrease in covered bond yields and spreads, increasing the attractiveness of covered bond funding.

With regards to bank capital market funding, Caruana and van Rixtel (2011, p. 2) report the GFC to have led to "major changes in the composition of gross bond issuance instruments [...]. The share of covered bonds [...] has increased from 26% in the first half of 2007 to 40% and 45% in the first half of 2010 and 2012, respectively." Despite capital market sources anecdotally reporting an increase in emission activity due to CBPP1 (Burmeister, 2009; Winkler, 2009), only Beirne et al. (2011) structurally evaluate the impact of covered bond purchases in the primary market. Their cointegration analysis finds covered bonds to crowd out unsecured bonds.

This leads to the question, whether the change in banks' funding structure identified by Caruana and van Rixtel (2011) and the increase in covered bond emission volumes suggested by Beirne et al. (2011) are attributable to changing market conditions and regulation, or driven by the Eurosystem's interventions. In case of the latter, only eurozone markets should be affected, while both, eurozone and non-eurozone markets, would be subject to the former.

In this section, we contribute to the literature by determining the additional covered bond emission volume attributable to the covered bond purchases of the Eurosystem, while controlling for bank funding conditions. Additionally, we distinguish between core and periphery markets, and infer causality via a difference-in-difference estimator.

4.1 Data and Methodology

We aggregate a rich dataset of individual covered bond emissions from 2007Q1 to 2015Q2, obtained from Thomson Reuters SDC Platinum, by quarter and by country. CBPP volumes were retrieved from the ECB and all additional data points from Thompson Reuters Datastream and the European Mortgage Federation (EMF).

We consider the covered bond market in an isolated fashion. Therefore, additional covered bond emission volumes triggered by the CBPPs are regarded a success towards the ECB's primary goal of easing bank funding conditions. To infer the causal relationship between the CBPPs and emission volumes, we employ a difference-in-difference estimator within a fixed effects regression and correct for autocorrelation and heteroskedasticity (see Eq. 1). Denmark, Norway, Sweden, and the United Kingdom serve as our control group, for which we assume funding conditions to resemble those of the eurozone. To capture differences within the eurozone, we divide our sample into core and periphery countries for the latter part of our analysis.[45]

$$EV_{i,t} = \alpha + \beta_1^{'} X_{i,t} + \beta_2 \sum_{n=1}^{3} CBPP_{n,i,t} + \beta_3 Ez \times \sum_{n=1}^{3} CBPP_{n,i,t} + \mu_i + \epsilon_{i,t} \qquad (1)$$

The absolute volume of covered bond emissions $EV_{i,t}$ per country i and quarter t serves as our dependent variable. Vector $\boldsymbol{X}_{i,t}$ represents a set of control variables (Table 7) and the difference-in-difference estimator consists of the interaction term of the policy intervention $CBPP_{n,i,t}$ and a dummy for eurozone countries, *Ez*. μ_i represents country fixed effects.

Table 7: Descriptive Statistics

	N	Range	Percentile			Mean	Std. Dev.
			5th	Median	95th		
Emission Volume	373	75.8	0.0	3.3	29.5	7.2	10.0
Swap Rate	373	5.1	0.3	1.5	4.6	1.7	1.2
Covered Bond Swap Spread	373	11.9	-0.1	0.8	4.4	1.3	1.5
House Price Index	373	96.4	63.6	100.5	132.0	99.6	18.2
Banking Sector Risk	373	9.4	0.8	2.2	5.8	2.7	1.8

As the measure for policy intervention $CBPP_{n,i,t}$, we employ the specific purchase volume for each country and quarter.[46] However, we note that the mechanism according to which the Eurosystem distributed its covered bond purchases is unknown (Gibson et al., 2015).[47] We therefore assume that they were undertaken in line with total emission supply. We define our $CBPP_{n,i,t}$ measure as the total euro-amount of the Eurosystem's interventions over the

[45] Core countries: Austria, Finland, France, and Germany, Netherlands; periphery countries: Ireland, Italy, Portugal, and Spain.

[46] We also tested for dummies as our $CBPP_{n,i,t}$ measure, which led to similarly structured regression coefficients in terms of sign and significance, but yielded an unrealistically high estimate of €160 billion in covered bond emissions attributable to CBPP1.

[47] The ECB capital key is explicitly not employed, but the risks of CBPP3 are shared according the ECB capital key. Under the FAQ for CBPP3, the ECB (2015b) merely states that "decisions on the allocation of particular purchases to its members take due account of their specific competencies."

share of total emission volumes per country as published by the EMF. For the purpose of employing a difference-in-difference estimator, we assign a fictional intervention value to our control group, which assumes these countries had been part of the eurozone and the intervention volume had been proportionally larger.

We include two control variables to capture the absolute pricing levels in covered bond markets and the attractiveness of covered bond funding. The *Swap Rate* for each country at the maturity equivalent to the Markit iBoxx covered bond index of the same period is complemented by the difference between the yield of this very index and the previously mentioned swap rate (*Covered Bond Swap Spread*). These two measures also capture sovereign credit risk, which is a component of covered bond prices.

We additionally control for the difficulty of banks attaining capital market funding, via the *Banking Sector Risk* measure. This is defined as the difference between the Markit iBoxx subordinated and senior unsecured index yields.[48] The *House Price Index* is the final control variable, representing the ability to emit additional covered bonds and the development of the bonds' collateral value (Prokopczuk & Vonhoff, 2012).

Finally, we account for unobserved time varying effects by introducing two specifications of time dummy variables. First, we employ *Quarter of Year Dummies* (specification B) to accommodate for the fact that banks do typically not distribute their emission activity evenly throughout the year but tend to frontload funding. Second, we use individual *Quarter Dummies* to capture any time-varying trend in covered bond emission markets, including banking sector risk and investor sentiment (specification C).

4.2 Results

The results of our estimations are presented in Table 8 to Table 9. We find the *Swap Rate* to be positively and the *Banking Sector Risk* to be negatively correlated with covered bond emission activity. The latter is absorbed by the *Quarter Dummies* under specification C.

Our results build on the actual intervention volumes per country as our $CBPP_{n,i,t}$ measure and the emission volume per country as our dependent varia-

[48] A number of further risk measures with respect to interbank stress, funding conditions and sovereign debt crisis have been tested but did not materially improve the results.

ble. Since they are in common units, the interaction term can be interpreted as a marginal emission effect of the CBPPs. More precisely, it depicts the average additional emission volume per euro billion in Eurosystem purchases.

We find each euro billion in interventions to have triggered an additional €6.3 to 6.9 billion in covered bond emissions during CBPP1 (Table 8). Considering the total intervention volume of €16.2 billion, we derive an additional aggregate emission activity of €103 to 112 billion, which is equivalent to 69% of all eligible covered bond emissions undertaken during CBPP1 (ECB, 2010). We are therefore able to confirm anecdotal evidence of CBPP1 having triggered increased covered bond emission activity.

Table 8: Emission Volume Regression Results

	(1) A	(2) B	(3) C
$CBPP1_{i,t}$	-1.55	-1.90	-1.75
$CBPP2_{i,t}$	7.33	5.67	0.63
$CBPP3_{i,t}$	0.53	0.40	0.10
$CBPP1_{i,t}$ × Eurozone	6.80*	6.85*	6.32*
$CBPP2_{i,t}$ × Eurozone	0.50	0.01	-1.34
$CBPP3_{i,t}$ × Eurozone	-0.65	-0.81	-2.08
$Swap\ Rate_{i,t}$	3.03***	2.98***	8.70***
$Covered\ Bond\ Swap\ Spread_{i,t}$	0.44	0.48	0.10
$Banking\ Sector\ Risk_t$	-0.74***	-0.72***	
$House\ Price\ Index_{i,t}$	-0.05	-0.05	-0.08
$Quarter\ of\ Year\ Dummy_t$	no	yes	no
$Quarter\ Dummy_t$	no	no	yes
Constant	8.51	10.12*	-11.51
Observations	373	373	373
Groups	13	13	13
Coefficient of Determination (R^2)	0.201	0.221	0.295
Log-Likelihood	-1258	-1253	-1235
Akaike Information Criterion (AIC)	2536	2531	2493
Bayesian Information Criterion (BIC)	2575	2578	2540

Estimation of CBPP impact on country-level covered bond emission volumes for 9 eurozone countries using a control group of 4 non-eurozone countries. Estimates are calculated via an autocorrelation and heteroskedasticity corrected panel fixed effects regression. The intervention measure takes the shape of the total purchases per country and quarter under the respective CBPP in euro billion. The difference-in-difference interaction terms represent the emission volume attributable to the Eurosystem's intervention. The sample period is from 2007Q1 to 2015Q2. Significance levels: * 0.10, ** 0.05, *** 0.01.

Neither for CBPP2, nor for CBPP3, are we able to attribute any additional covered bond emission volume to the Eurosystem's interventions. According to

Sarafana (2012), banks might have drawn sufficient liquidity from the ECB's LTRO2 in late 2011, decreasing the relevance of CBPP2.

Separating the impact of the Eurosystem's purchase programs between core and periphery countries (Table 9), we note a slightly lower marginal emission effect for core countries than previously mentioned of 5.4 to 5.7x. The coefficient turns insignificant when *Quarter Dummies* are included (specification C). On the contrary, we estimate a highly significant marginal emission effect of 14.3x for periphery countries. This suggests CBPP1 having had the largest impact on the most fragile markets. Of these, Ireland and Spain have been subject to severe real estate crises and banking sector turmoil. The resumed primary covered bond market was therefore able to provide long-term funding. Again, programs two and three remained without an effect.

Our analysis depends on the degree of market coverage of the dataset employed. SDC covers emissions in the public domain, for which data was made available by issuers or underwriters. We assume to cover the whole universe of public covered bond emissions, while eligibility criteria of the ECB reduce the investable universe, which likely leads to an underestimation of our results. The opposite effect can be attributed to our omission of private placements and retained issues. The latter became popular since 2011Q3 (Caruana & van Rixtel, 2011; Jobst, 2015), and might have influenced our results for CBPP2 and CBPP3. While high quality covered bonds could be pledged as collateral for repo transactions with the ECB during CBPP2, CBPP3 explicitly allowed for the purchase of retained covered bond issues.

Table 9: Emission Volume Regression Results with Regional Sample Split

	(4) A	(5) B	(6) C
$CBPP1_{i,t}$	-1.59	-1.94	-0.82
$CBPP2_{i,t}$	7.30	5.66	0.79
$CBPP3_{i,t}$	0.53	0.40	0.11
$CBPP1_{i,t}$ × *Eurozone* × *Core*	5.64*	5.73*	5.35
$CBPP2_{i,t}$ × *Eurozone* × *Core*	2.32	1.98	0.09
$CBPP3_{i,t}$ × *Eurozone* × *Core*	-1.00	-1.21	-2.20
$CBPP1_{i,t}$ × *Eurozone* × *Periphery*	15.56***	15.33***	14.25***
$CBPP2_{i,t}$ × *Eurozone* × *Periphery*	-2.13	-2.92	-3.45
$CBPP3_{i,t}$ × *Eurozone* × *Periphery*	0.00	-0.10	-1.76
$Swap\ Rate_{i,t}$	3.03***	2.98***	7.27***
$Covered\ Bond\ Swap\ Spread_{i,t}$	0.51	0.56	0.18
$Banking\ Sector\ Risk_t$	-0.77***	-0.75***	
$House\ Price\ Index_{i,t}$	-0.06	-0.06	-0.08
$Quarter\ of\ Year\ Dummy_t$	no	yes	no
$Quarter\ Dummy_t$	no	no	yes
Constant	8.90	10.44*	-5.44
Observations	373	373	373
Groups	13	13	13
Coefficient of Determination (R^2)	0.208	0.228	0.300
Log-Likelihood	-1256	-1251	-1233
Akaike Information Criterion (AIC)	2536	2527	2491
Bayesian Information Criterion (BIC)	2583	2574	2538

Estimation of CBPP impact on country-level covered bond emission volumes for 5 core and 4 periphery eurozone countries using a control group of 4 non-eurozone countries. Estimates are calculated via an autocorrelation and heteroskedasticity corrected panel fixed effects regression. The intervention measure takes the shape of the total purchases per country and quarter under the respective CBPP in euro billion. The difference-in-difference interaction terms represent the emission volume attributable to the Eurosystem's intervention. The sample period is from 2007Q1 to 2015Q2. Significance levels: * 0.10, ** 0.05, *** 0.01.

4.3 Subsidiary Conclusion

Employing an aggregated dataset of covered bond emissions in Europe, we quantify the additional covered bond emission volume attributable to the three Eurosystem's CBPPs versus a control group of four non-eurozone covered bond markets. We find an increased emission activity triggered by CBPP1, which we estimate at a multiple of 6.8x of the intervention volume employed by the Eurosystem. The total additional emission volume of €103 billion is equivalent to approximately 69% of all eligible bonds emitted during the time of the program. The program has therefore been successful in re-establishing a functional primary covered bond market and thereby enabled banks to obtain capital market funding to maintain and increase their stock of loans to the economy.

This effect is even stronger for periphery countries with a marginal effect of 14.3x. The program has therefore provided the greatest relief to banking sectors in countries, of which some were subject to the greatest real estate bubbles within the eurozone. On the contrary, we do not find additional emission volumes triggered by the second and third program, which were introduced at a time of relatively sound covered bond market conditions.

We therefore conclude CBPPs to be effective in stimulating covered bond funding, only when capital markets are stalling due to a stressed banking sector, which was the case for CBPP1.

5 Medium-term Impact on the Secondary Market[49]

Covered bonds are an important vehicle for long-term funding of mortgages and present a safe investment due to their dual recourse structure. The latter is the main reason they trade at only a slight premium over sovereign bonds, and provide banks cheap access to mortgage funding. The covered bond market has been considered impeccable in terms of both, risk and pricing (e.g., Anand, Chapman, & Gai, 2012). However, the GFC has led to a re-assessment of the risk-profile inherent in covered bonds and consequently to reduced market access for low-quality issuers and sovereigns. Overall, however, the market remained sound and was able to provide funding to the banking system at all times during the GFC.

In 2009, the Eurosystem decided to improve the re-financing conditions for banks in its member countries. The objective was to reinvigorate inter-bank lending, in particular involving those banks that had largely been cut off from refinancing due to soaring sovereign risk in the wake of the GFC. The chosen intervention of outright bond purchases was targeted at the covered bond market because this market is (a) central to the refinancing needs of banks and (b) large enough to absorb the sizable amounts of resources required for central bank intervention.

In this section, we re-assess the effectiveness of the CBPP1 and establish the effectiveness the two subsequent programs on secondary markets. We measure effectiveness in terms of the tightening of covered bond yields of Eurozone issuers, which benefit from purchases under the CBPPs versus those from the United Kingdom, which do not. We employ an unobserved components modeling strategy and some more conventional modeling approaches as robustness checks. The analysis extends the available literature, such as Beirne et al. (2011), in terms of methodology, by including the last two purchase programs, and by determining the duration of the programs' effectiveness.

The results of Beirne et al. (2011) for CBPP1 can generally be confirmed in that we find a 10 to 11-bp tightening of covered bond spreads upon the announcement of the targeted Eurosystem purchase program. The yield spread is

---

49 This Section is co-authored by Joachim Zietz.

H. Markmann, *Covered Bonds under Unconventional Monetary Policy*,
Essays in Real Estate Research 14,
https://doi.org/10.1007/978-3-658-20975-9_5

measured against euro-denominated covered bonds issued by banks headquartered in the United Kingdom. The tightening of the spread lasts for approximately seven weeks. For CBPP2 and CBPP3, the results are mixed, with a tendency for a lower impact. However, we note in this context that the framework of the latter two intervention programs is less clear-cut than that of the first. Also, capital markets had by then attained knowledge of the functioning of CBPPs and acted selectively. The volume of covered bonds purchased by the Eurosystem tends to exhibit a positive correlation with covered bond yield spreads.

The remainder of the section is organized as follows. Sub-section 2 provides an overview of the Eurosystem's CBPPs and insights into the market environment under which the programs were initiated. The following section covers previous work on the topic, while Section 4 describes the dataset employed. Sub-section 5 provides the methodology that is used to generate the results presented in Sub-section 6. Sub-section 7 concludes this section.

5.1 Literature

In the months running up to the second quarter of 2009, the spreads between euro-denominated covered bonds and interest swaps widened substantially; primary issuance activity came to a near halt and credit markets tightened substantially. This intensification of the financial crisis led the way for market participants to call for an intervention by the Eurosystem along the lines of the unconventional monetary policy measures of the U.S. Federal Reserve and the Bank of England.[50]

In its May 2009 monthly meeting, the ECB Governing Council decided to implement a covered bond purchase program, under which a targeted volume of €60 billion in covered bonds would be acquired in outright market acquisitions. This program marked one of the first unconventional monetary policy actions by the Eurosystem and caught market participants by surprise (Beirne et al., 2011; Szczerbowicz, 2015). One of the key objectives of CBPP1 was to promote a depression of covered bond yields and an increased lending activity via an easing of funding conditions. The hope was that the program would help mitigate the "exceptional" market conditions (ECB, 2009, p. 18).

---

50 See Rogers, Scotti, and Wright (2014) for an overview of unconventional monetary policy measures by the Federal Reserve, Bank of England, Bank of Japan, and the ECB.

A month later, the ECB announced that euro-denominated, investment grade bonds with a value of at least €500 million would be acquired, as long as their issuers were based in the Eurozone and the instruments were UCITS compliant or otherwise qualified as collateral for ECB operations. Additionally, the Eurosystem would acquire bonds via its Member Central Banks in primary and secondary markets for the 12-month period from July 2009 to June 2010 (ECB, 2009). Ex post, the Eurosystem had acquired covered bonds in the amount of €43.8 billion in the secondary and €16.2 billion in the primary market, which translates into an absorption rate of 10.8% of all new eligible issues for this time period (ECB, 2010). A detailed overview of all CBPP characteristics is shown in Table 10.

During the course of 2010, the covered bond market had largely recovered, but became more fragmented, as the sovereign debt crisis emerged. In order to diminish the arising funding difficulties, the ECB intended to support lending activity, particularly in peripheral member countries by ensuring bank liquidity (Packmohr & Weigerding, 2015). In October 2010, the ECB Governing Council announced a second CBPP with a target volume of €40 billion. This had largely been discussed and anticipated. Since the covered bond market was in a rather healthy shape, which had triggered numerous primary market issues immediately before the announcement (Credit Suisse, 2011), it was considered uncertain whether CBPP2 would be able to reach its goals.

The technical details of CBPP2 largely mimic those of CBPP1, except for the lower target volume, a lower minimum amount for an issue (€300 million), an extension of the maturity window from zero to 10.5 years, and a lower rating requirement (BBB-) (ECB, 2011). All told, the Eurosystem acquired a total of 37% in the primary and 63% in the secondary market. However, its targeted purchase volume of €40 billion was not reached; only €16 billion worth of covered bonds were purchased.

At the time of the third CBPP, the covered bond market did not show any signs of weakness that would have required a Eurosystem intervention. The program was introduced instead to accomplish macroeconomic goals, such as credit provision, central bank balance sheet management and inflation management (Packmohr & Weigerding, 2015; Dunne et al. 2015). Covered bonds were only one of numerous private sector asset classes used for intervention purposes (Packmohr & Weigerding, 2015; Draghi, 2014). In fact, all market participants were surprised by the ECB Governing Council's announcement to include covered bonds in the widely expected purchase program.

Table 10: Overview of CBPP1 to CBPP3 Characteristics

	CBPP1	CBPP2	CBPP3
Volume	€60bn	€40bn (only €16bn realized)	initially not specified (later €10bn per month, including ABSPP)
Announcement	07/05/2009	06/10/2011	04/09/2014
Technical details	04/06/2009	03/11/2011	02/10/2014
Period	07/2009 - 06/2010	11/2011 - 10/2012	10/2014 - 09/2016, potentially later
Eligible issuers	Eurozone banks	Eurozone banks	Eurozone banks & Multi-Cédulas SPVs
Eligible instruments	UCITS compliant or similarly structured CBs eligible for ECB Repos	UCITS compliant or similarly structured CBs eligible for ECB Repos	Eligible for ECB Repos + Multi-Cédulas
Eligible currencies	EUR only	EUR only	EUR only
Bond size	≥ €500m (exceptionally > €100m)	≥ €300m	not specified
Time to Maturity	3-7 years	< 10.5 years	not specified
Rating requirement	At least AA (exceptionally BBB-)	At least BBB-	At least BBB-, (exceptions for CY and GR)
Purchase limit	Not specified	Not specified	≤ 70% per ISIN (aggregated across CBPP1 to CBPP3)
Market Segments	Primary & Secondary	Primary & Secondary	Primary & Secondary, retained papers explicitly included
Share Primary / Secondary	27% / 73%	37% / 63%	18% / 82% (June 2015)

Source: Adapted from Packmohr and Weigerding (2015, p. 22)

Building on the previous programs, the purchase requirements for CBPP3 were further relaxed: Spanish Multi-Cédulas became eligible, the rating requirement was reduced for issues from Cyprus and Greece, and fully retained papers were explicitly included in the scope of eligible issues (ECB, 2014). Although initially not mentioned, the monthly purchase volume of covered bonds and asset-backed securities turned out to be about €10 billion, of which only 18% were comprised of covered bonds acquired in the primary market up to June 2015. The cumulative volume of covered bonds purchased under each of the three programs can be found in Figure 12.[51]

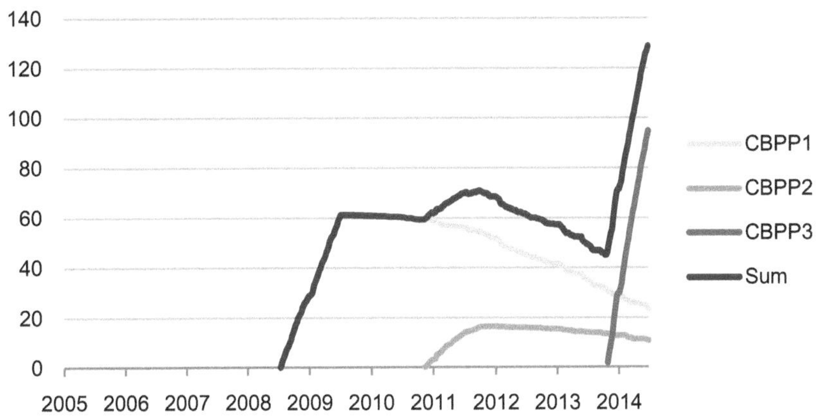

Figure 12: Cumulative CBPP Purchases on ECB Balance Sheet
Including end of quarter adjustments and amortization. Source: Own Illustration based on ECB (2015b)

While we have only described CBPPs up to this point, it has to be made clear that the Eurosystem also employed a variety of other conventional and unconventional monetary policy instruments.[52]

Beirne et al. (2011) provide an analysis of the economic background of CBPP1 and the primary and secondary market effects. For the primary market analysis, they employ a co-integration technique and conclude that the program has revived the primary covered bond market, although at the expense of the

[51] The decay in the graphs is due to maturing bonds, as the Eurosystem does not sell covered bonds on the secondary market.

[52] These include forward guidance, the SMP, the TLTRO and the ABSPP. For a summary of the ECB's policy tool box and its use, refer to Pattipeilohy et al. (2013).

unsecured bank bond market. In their secondary market analysis, Beirne et al. (2011) perform a descriptive yield analysis indicating a spread tightening at the CBPP1 announcement. The average yield tightening amounts to 12 bps for Eurozone bonds for the period after the announcement of the first CBPP. Similar effects could be found for Germany (-17 bps), France (-10 bps), and Spain (-17 bps). A non-significant announcement effect is found only for Ireland.

Most of the studies on the impact of unconventional monetary policy in general and the covered bond purchase programs in particular focus on their effects on sovereign bond yields and employ event study techniques. Falagiarda and Reitz (2015) is a recent example; the authors find no significant average or cumulative announcement effect for CBPP1 and CBPP2. The insignificant effect of CBPP announcements on sovereign yield spreads is shared by Watfe (2015) and Kilponen et al. (2015). By contrast, Rivolta (2014) finds a general tightening of sovereign bond spreads upon the announcement of unconventional monetary policies, including the announcements of CBPP1 and CBPP2 announcements. Szczerbowicz (2015) determines this tightening to amount to 6 to 7 bps for the Euribor/OIS and Euribor/Bund spreads.

The impact of unconventional monetary policy is also studied for assets other than sovereign bonds, such as commercial bank CDS, and more general economic indicators, such as inflation. Gerlach-Kristen (2015), for example, finds individual bank default risks to decrease with the purchases of covered bonds by the Eurosystem. Peersman (2011) shows that unconventional monetary policy actions stimulate economic activity and raise inflation in the Euro area economy. De Pooter, DeSimone, Martin, and Pruitt (2015) identify large announcement effects but almost no implementation effects for the SMP. Fawley and Neely (2013) find mixed results for the CBPP and LTRO monetary expansion.

Similar to the Eurosystem's CBPP, the Swiss National Bank initiated an outright bond purchase program in 2009, without specifically referring to covered bonds or any target volume. Considering these differences, Kettemann and Krogstrup (2013) find a 10-bp tightening of covered bond spreads against sovereign debt. However, due to the different circumstances, it cannot be determined whether this effect is due to the announcement or the actual implementation of the program.

Only recently, two studies have considered the immediate effect of the Eurosystem's CBPPs on the target asset class of covered bonds. Szczerbowicz (2015) finds the announcements of CBPP1 and CBPP2 jointly to lead to a long-term tightening of covered bond spreads versus German Bunds of 4 bps for each program.[53] Most importantly, however, she finds a larger impact of outright sovereign bond purchases on covered bond spreads than of outright covered bond purchases, which she attributes to the large role of sovereign risk and banks as investors in sovereign bond markets. While the Szczerbowicz (2015) study considers daily spreads, Gibson et al. (2016) employ a monthly dataset in order to control for fundamental data and rating agency decisions. They also find a modest increase in covered bond prices for the five stressed countries: Greece, Ireland, Italy, Portugal, and Spain. This holds true even more strongly for longer maturities.

Anand et al. (2012) consider the secondary market spread decline and strong increase in primary market bond issuances as proof of their model. Relating to their own study on bond market liquidity, Schuster and Uhrig-Homburg (2014) find a similar effect in that the 12-bp tightening translates into a 2 bp change per €10 billion liquidity injection for CBPP1.[54] Falagiarda and Reitz (2015) confirm Beirne et al.'s (2011) finding that the efficient market hypothesis holds for the covered bond markets; they question the cost efficiency of the first CBPP.

5.2 Data and Methodology

We use weekly (Friday) data for European covered bond benchmark indexes, as assembled by Markit's iBoxx series, for the time period from January 2006 to June 2015. The data are from Thomson Reuters Datastream and span the pre-crisis, crisis, and post-crisis periods, which includes the announcement and implementation of the Eurosystem's CBPPs (Figure 10).[55]

---

[53] The spread changes for the individual countries amount to -4 bps for France, -5 bps for Germany, -10 bps for Italy, and -6 bps for Spain. The results for Portugal are not significant; the announcement of CBPP1 had a widening and the announcement of CBPP2 a tightening effect on Irish covered bond spreads.

[54] For reference, Eser and Schwab (2015) find an approximate 3-bp tightening for a 1/1000 purchase of the outstanding debt for the SMP.

[55] We note that only the first eight months of the implementation of CBPP3 are covered.

To enter an iBoxx-index, covered bonds need to have a minimum time to maturity of 1 year, a minimum amount outstanding of €500 million, and be assigned an average investment grade rating from Fitch, Moody's, or Standard & Poor's. The indexes used in this study only reflect euro-denominated covered bonds. They include those for the overall euro-market, Germany, France, Spain, Ireland, and the United Kingdom. Each index is volume weighted and rebalanced on a monthly basis.

It has to be noted in this context that there exists no dedicated index for bond issuers that are located in the Eurozone. The Euro-market benchmark index that is employed in this study also comprises a small number of bonds issued by institutions based in countries such as the United Kingdom, USA, New Zealand, Switzerland and Australia. However, since bond issues from non-Euro countries make up only a small share of the index, it can serve as a proxy for developments in the Eurozone.[56] On this basis, the dependent variables are defined as the difference between the index-yield for the Eurozone, or a particular country from the Eurozone and the index-yield for euro-denominated covered bonds issued by banks based in the United Kingdom (Figure 13).

Datastream serves as the source for numerous money-market variables used in this study, such as the respective country sovereign bond yields, the Euro Overnight Index Swap rates, the Euro-Libor Swap rates, and the sovereign bond yields. To match the approximate average maturity of the covered bonds under considerations,[57] these instruments also relate to a five-year reference maturity. The same holds true for other variables, such as the Eurostoxx 50 Volatility Index (VSTOXX) and the European Financial Institutions Senior Bond CDS. The ECB (2015b) serves as the source for the Eurosystem's purchase volumes for the covered bond purchase programs, as displayed in Figure 12.

The weekly changes of the iBoxx index for the Eurozone (Figure 14) indicate an increase in market volatility in November of 2007, which lasts until the beginning of 2014, when the dispersion of weekly yield changes decreases notably. Similarly, the spread between the European indexes, including Spain's, has

---

[56] This approximation is in line with Beirne et al. (2011); Szczerbowicz (2015) remains unclear on this matter. As of June 2015, the proportion of euro-denominated covered bonds by issuers not based in the Eurozone was approximately 15%, of which approximately 6.4% are attributable to the United Kingdom.

[57] As of June 2015, Markit iBoxx descriptive statistics depict maturity of 4.9 years.

strongly tightened and seems to be trading at constant levels since March 2014. This view is confirmed by the graphical representation of the yield differences in Figure 13. The data at hand therefore represents the complete cycle of the GFC's impact on European covered bond markets. Accordingly, we are in a position to answer a number of interesting questions about the covered bond behavior during the crisis period.

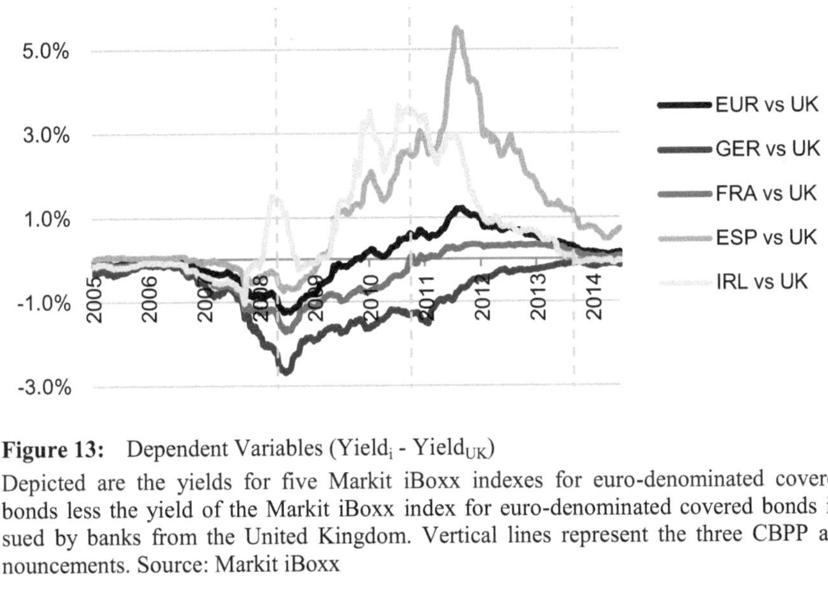

Figure 13: Dependent Variables ($Yield_i$ - $Yield_{UK}$)

Depicted are the yields for five Markit iBoxx indexes for euro-denominated covered bonds less the yield of the Markit iBoxx index for euro-denominated covered bonds issued by banks from the United Kingdom. Vertical lines represent the three CBPP announcements. Source: Markit iBoxx

With the onset of the GFC, covered bond spreads between different countries widened and started to partly represent the credit worthiness of the local banking sector. This trend lasted until October 2010, when the European sovereign crisis further drove continental European covered bond yields. By this time, the yield difference between Eurozone and British covered bonds inversed, with British ones being perceived more secure. German covered bonds, which claimed safe-haven status, kept a lower yield all throughout.

Typically, unconventional monetary policy can be analyzed in terms of announcement effects, rate levels, and outright market purchase volumes. It turns out that unconventional monetary policy has its strongest impact at the time of its announcement, for which event study methodologies are the method of choice.

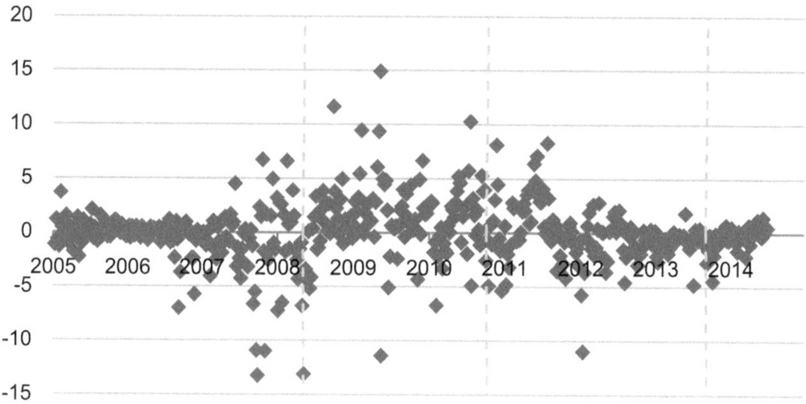

Figure 14: Scatter Plot of Period Changes for $Yield_{Eurozone}$ - $Yield_{UK}$
The daily changes are depicted in basis points. Shown are weekly changes of the difference the between the overall and the British Markit iBoxx indexes for euro-denominated covered bonds. Source: Own illustration based on Markit iBoxx

Previous event studies on unconventional monetary policy include numerous methodological approaches. Rivolta (2014) employs two-sided t-tests on 2-day event windows around an announcement, as developed by Swanson (2011). This is closely matched by Altavilla, Giannone, and Lenza's (2016) use of an F-test to determine the significance of the first difference in the changes for a two-day event window. Kilponen et al. (2015) employ a first-differences regression for yield spreads for 2- and 3-day windows; this is similar to Fratzscher et al.'s (2014) first differences on one-day event windows. Kettemann and Krogstrup (2013) employ a distributed lag model with 3 lags of the issue dummy on first differences.

Gagnon et al. (2011) employ an out-of-sample forecasting approach and thereby follow the methodology proposed by Backus and Wright (2007). Szczerbowicz (2015) estimate an AR(1)-model on 2-day event windows. Similarly, Gibson et al. (2016) use an ARMAX model in combination with time and country fixed effects. Watfe (2015) employs a GARCH model with two-day event windows and Peersman (2011) resorts to a VAR-model. Finally, Joyce et al. (2011) combine the latter two approaches and employ VAR and GARCH-M models for a quantity based framework of British quantitative easing measures.

The current study deviates from the previous ones in that it relies on an unobserved components model (UCM), which is also known as a structural time series model.[58] The basic idea is to parameterize an unobservable trend, seasonal influences or other components in a very flexible manner that allows for variation in these components over time and obviates the need for pre-testing for stationarity in the mean or season. Allowing for stochastic components typically improves the fit and often also allows one to capture the impact of omitted variables.[59] Its most basic form, the local level model, consists of the two equations

$$y_t = \mu_t + \beta X_t + \epsilon_t \tag{2}$$

$$\mu_t = \mu_{t-1} + \eta_t \tag{3}$$

where ε_t and η_t are assumed normally distributed, independent and identically distributed (IID) and are mutually independent of one another.

The constant term typically present in OLS regressions is replaced in Equation (1) by the stochastic trend term μ_t, which is specified in Equation (2) as as a random walk.[60] The random walk component allows for non-stationarity in Equation (1). This is sufficient to capture temporary spikes in the dependent variable, but not systematic growth in the dependent variable over time.

The inclusion of the regression component, which consists of the vector of regressors $\mathbf{X}_t$ and its associated coefficient vector β, offers an additional perspective on the model: It explicitly decomposes the dependent variable into an observed component, that is vector $\mathbf{X}_t$ and an unobserved component μ_t.

Unobserved component models sometimes fail to converge because the data are not rich enough to allow for a separate estimation of two or more variance

---

58 The UCM is a special case of state space modeling, which was introduced into the economics and finance literature by Harvey (1989). See Harvey (1997), Durbin and Koopman (2001) and Commandeur and Koopman (2007) for more detail on the UCM approach. See Zietz and Trajan (2014) and Füss and Zietz (2016) for recent applications of UCMs to return series.

59 Omitted variables may arise in typical regression applications because the underlying theory is not specific enough to identify all relevant variables or not all variables that are mandated by the relevant theory are available.

60 If the variance of μ_t is statistically insignificant from zero (which can be tested via a likelihood ratio test), the random walk collapses to a constant term ($\mu_t = \mu_{t-1} = \mu$) just as in least squares regression.

terms, which also turned out to be the case in the present application. This problem can be overcome by reducing the number of variances to be estimated while still keeping the random walk attribute.[61] A simple solution is to set the variance of the term ε_t in Equation (1) equal to zero, which results in the following UCM system,[62]

$$y_t = \mu_t + \beta X_t \quad (4)$$

$$\mu_t = \mu_{t-1} + \eta_t \quad (5)$$

Covered bonds issued by British financial institutions are not subject to the Eurosystem's CBPPs, as the Bank of England is not part of the Eurosystem and such covered bonds are therefore not eligible for purchases under any CBPP. Since there exists a sufficiently large sample of euro-denominated covered bonds issued by British financial institutions, we use the respective iBoxx index to construct a difference-in-difference estimator. For that purpose, we employ the difference between the yield of all euro-denominated covered bonds (or of the respective countries under consideration) $y_{countryi,t}$ and those issued by British financial institutions[63] $y_{UK,t}$ as our dependent variable. Our key identifying assumption is that the covered bonds issued by financial institutions from the Eurozone and the United Kingdom behave the same under regular market conditions. Having the difference between Eurozone and UK bond yields on the left obviates the need to model underlying bond market level variations caused by exogenous factors.

The yield difference appears to follow a random walk, which is confirmed by unit-root testing, which identifies its I(1)-property (see Appendix 2). The UCM model of Equations (3) and (4) easily captures the I(1)-property of the dependent variables. What makes the UCM approach particularly useful in this context is the fact that the individual components of the two bond indexes at the

61 Various model specifications were tested, of which the simple random walk specification of the UCM with only one variance term provides a sufficient representation of the data generating process.

62 The model may easily be expanded to include cycle, seasonal, and trend data. See, for example, Pelagatti (2015).

63 The analysis does not mitigate the above mentioned selection bias. However, this only results in a smoothing effect in difference of the yields. In using the respective covered bond index in constructing the dependent variable, we build on Szczerbowicz (2015), who employs individual country spreads versus Germany.

core of this analysis are unavailable, while the bond market sentiment cannot be fully captured with the observed regressors at hand.

Equation (5) of Model A contains on the left-hand side the difference between the covered bond yield of a particular Eurozone country and the corresponding yield of bonds issued by British banks. We recall that the British bonds are not purchased by the Eurosystem and can, therefore, serve as our counterfactual.

Model A: Average Impact Model

$$y_{country,t} - y_{UK,t} = \mu_t + \beta'_1 X_t + \sum_{j=1}^{3} \delta_{2,j} CBPP_{Ann_{j,t}} + \sum_{j=1}^{3} \delta_{3,j} CBPP_{Vol_{j,t}} \tag{6}$$

$$\mu_t = \mu_{t-1} + \eta_t \tag{7}$$

where η_t is IID normally distributed.

We control for a number of variables contained in X_t. In particular, vector X contains five regressors. One of these regressors is the spread between the five-year Euro overnight index swap (OIS) and the five-year libor-euro swap *(OIS vs Libor Spread)* to account for differences in the euro- and pound money markets. Tensions in the European financial system are controlled for by the average spread of the five-year government yields for Italy, Portugal, Ireland, and Spain versus the five-year government yield for Germany (*Avg. IPSI Spread*).[64] This second measure is capable of reflecting the various stages of the sovereign debt crises with different countries in the focal point. Another control variable is the iTraxx Senior Financial CDS-index (*iTraxx Senior Financial*); it is meant to reflect stress in the banking industry. The difference between the 3 and 7 year interest rates for the United Kingdom (*UK 3-7yrs IRS*) and each country under consideration (*Country$_i$ 3-7yrs IRS*) are the fourth and fifth control variables.

CBPP_Ann$_j$, for j = {1,2,3} is a dummy variable that equals zero before the announcement and one for all weeks after the announcement of the respective CBPP. We also employ an alternative definition, where the dummy variable is one only up to the end of the implementation of the program. This approach builds on the assumption that purchase volumes are an endogenous market stim-

[64] Alternatively, sovereign CDS quotes have been employed but do not provide for better results and are subject to availability inconsistencies.

ulus, which has no lasting effect on market spreads when abolished. We also determine the impact of the actual open market purchase volumes of covered bonds $CBPP\_Vol_{j,t}$, as published by the ECB and first analyzed by Gibson et al. (2016). We are not able to attribute the purchase volumes to individual markets and therefore refer to the amount on a European basis.

According to the semi-strong form of the Efficient Market Hypothesis, capital markets should price-in all public information as it becomes available. Therefore, it would be expected that pricing would change quickly as new information arrives. However, it remains unknown for how long this effect is active, or if it even diminishes very quickly. To determine the duration of the announcements effects, we specify a General Distributed Lag Model under the same UCM framework as for Equation (5):

Model B: General Distributed Lag Model

$$y_{country,t} - y_{UK,t} = \mu_t + \beta'_1 X_t + \sum_{j=1}^{3} \sum_{i=0}^{8} \delta_{2,j,i}\, CBPP\_Ann_{j,t-i} + \sum_{j=1}^{3} \delta_{3,j}\, CBPP\_Vol_{j,t} \tag{8}$$

$$\mu_t = \mu_{t-1} + \eta_t \tag{9}$$

where the independent variables X_t, and $CBPP\_Vol_{j,t}$ remain unchanged relative to Equation (5). The impact of the CBPP announcements is now measured via a modified version of the variable $CBPP\_Ann_{j,t-i}$, a series of nine dummy variables, one for the announcement week and one for each of the eight weeks following the announcements. As the data are weekly, the first dummy variable effectively measures a [-3,1]-day event window, as the CBPPs were announced on Thursdays. The average over all i of the coefficients $\delta_{2,i}$ in Equation (7) is comparable to the single coefficient $\delta_{2,i}$ in Equation (5).

5.3 Results

Table 11 provides the estimation results related to the average impact of the three bond purchase programs of the Eurosystem. The first column of results provides the average impact for all euro-denominated covered bonds, while the following four columns show the results for Germany, France, Spain, and Ireland.

The results confirm a general tightening effect of the announcement of CBPP1 of 11 bps for the Eurozone. At a country level, we observe the largest effect for German covered bonds with a tightening of 14 bps versus those of British issuers. French and Spanish covered bond differences tightened by 8-9 bps, while the Irish market is an outlier with a widening of 13 bps. The announcement of the program therefore sparked a general tightening of covered bond spreads, in the expectation of monetary policy stimulus.

Table 11: Average Impact of Announced and Actual Bond Purchases

	(7) EUR	(8) GER	(9) FRA	(10) ESP	(11) IRL
OIS vs Libor Spread	-0.006	0.022	0.025	-0.118	-0.079
Avg IPSI Spread	0.023***	-0.016**	-0.011*	0.075***	0.124***
iTraxx Senior Financial	0.415***	0.054	0.251*	1.029***	0.573
$Country_i$ 7-3yrs IRS	-0.041	-0.343***	-0.091	-0.067	0.001
United Kingdom 7-3yrs IRS	-0.061*	-0.066	-0.042	-0.011	-0.118
CBPP1 Ann.	-0.109***	-0.140***	-0.082***	-0.091***	0.125***
CBPP2 Ann.	0.010	0.043***	0.049***	0.013	0.020
CBPP3 Ann.	-0.015***	0.014***	0.009***	-0.071***	-0.076***
CBPP1 Volume	0.014***	0.011***	0.009**	0.026***	0.011
CBPP2 Volume	0.023*	0.014	0.018*	0.089*	-0.058**
CBPP3 Volume	0.002*	0.001	0.001	0.005*	-0.000
Observations	494	494	494	494	494
Log-Likelihood	1132	999	1087	646	500
AIC	-2246	-1980	-2156	-1275	-983
BIC	-2208	-1942	-2118	-1237	-945

Estimated with an Unobserved Component Model (UCM), with the system containing a random walk component, with the variance terms not reported (the variance of the observation model is insignificant, the opposite holds true for the variance of the random walk component); the CBPP announcements are represented by dummy variables that take the value of 0 before and of 1 after the announcement of the respective purchase programs and remain such until the end of the sample period; the observations cover the period from January 2, 2006 to June 26, 2015. Significance levels: * 0.10, ** 0.05, *** 0.01.

These results for CBPP1 are of the same direction as those of Beirne et al. (2011). The magnitudes differ by a maximum of 3 bps for the Eurozone and the two core countries, Germany and France. For the Spanish market our estimate is much lower (-10 bps); our estimate for the Irish market is larger (+8 bps).

The announcement of CBPP2 did not significantly affect yield differences for Eurozone covered bonds. The yield differences for Germany and France increased by 4-5 bps, and there is no effect for Spain and Ireland. The announcement of CBPP3 resulted in small positive, but significant changes of the spread difference for the Eurozone and for Germany and France. Yield differences for Spain and Ireland tightened more substantially, by 7-8 bps.

The actual purchases under CBPP1 widened the yield differences between 1 and 3 bps per Euro billion, with the changes being statistically insignificant for Ireland. A similar widening resulted for the purchases under CBPP2, except for Spain and Ireland. The yield differences turned much larger for Spain and larger and negative for Ireland. The asset purchases conducted under CBPP3 did not result in economically meaningful changes of the yield differences.

The economically and statistically significant reaction of the yield differences to the *Avg IPSI Spread* factor demonstrates the status of German and, to a lesser extent, French bonds as safe havens of the covered bond universe.

The level difference measured by the CBPP announcement dummy variables in Table 11 relates to the average level change after the announcements. This results in multiple announcement dummies being included in the regression at the same time for programs 2 and 3, which may influence and offset each other. Descriptive statistics (compare to Figure 13) also suggest that the yield differences tend to zero toward the beginning of 2014, while the covered bond market was not subject to the Eurosystem's intervention measures. The average announcement effect dummies would capture this time period, which is not attributable to CBPP announcements. To check the impact of this particular model specification we limit the announcement effect period to a 56-week window (the respective dummy variable is zero thereafter), which is equal to the time span from the initial announcement to the completion of the respective purchases[65]. It is also the time period considered by Beirne et al. (2011). Table 12 summarizes the results.

The change in the model specification (announcement dummy variables) leads to a reduction in the estimated announcement effects (Table 12). The CBPP1 program still has a tightening effect for the overall market and for Spain of 6 bps, which is still consistent with the Eurosystem's intention. But it is not as large as previously assumed. For CBPP2, there is only one statistically significant effect, a tightening of the Irish yield differences. The announcement effects

[65] Eight weeks from the announcement to the beginning of the implementation and 52 weeks for the actual purchases for CBPP1. The preparation period reduces to four weeks for CBPP2-3. For CBPP3, the sample ends before the 56 week window is completed.

of CBPP3 match those of the previous analysis. The influence of the actual purchases resembles that of the previous analysis for all programs.

Table 12: Unobserved Components Model with 56-Week Dummies

	(12) EUR	(13) GER	(14) FRA	(15) ESP	(16) IRL
OIS vs Libor Spread	-0.005	0.021	0.026	-0.118	-0.076
Avg IPSI Spread	0.023***	-0.015**	-0.010*	0.075***	0.124***
iTraxx Senior Financial	0.411***	0.047	0.243	1.023***	0.528
Country$_i$ 7-3yrs IRS	-0.049	-0.355***	-0.094	-0.066	0.001
United Kingdom 7-3yrs IRS	-0.058	-0.060	-0.040	-0.010	-0.119
CBPP1 Ann. 60 weeks	-0.060*	-0.060	-0.035	-0.055*	-0.039
CBPP2 Ann. 56 weeks	0.004	0.013	0.019	0.001	0.049**
CBPP3 Ann.	-0.015***	0.014***	0.009***	-0.071***	-0.076***
CBPP1 Volume	0.013***	0.010**	0.008**	0.025***	0.010
CBPP2 Volume	0.023*	0.014	0.018*	0.089*	-0.058**
CBPP3 Volume	0.001*	0.001	0.001	0.004*	-0.000
Observations	494	494	494	494	494
Log-Likelihood	1128	992	1083	646	500
AIC	-2235	-1963	-2144	-1270	-978
BIC	-2188	-1917	-2098	-1224	-932

Estimated with an Unobserved Component Model (UCM), with the system containing a random walk component, with the variance terms not reported (the variance of the observation model is insignificant, the opposite holds true for the variance of the random walk component); the CBPP announcements are represented by dummies which take the value of 0 before and 1 after the announcement of the respective purchase program for a total period of 56 weeks; the observation period is January 2, 2006 to June 26, 2015. Significance levels: * 0.10, ** 0.05, *** 0.01.

We finally employ a model that reflects the semi-strong form of the Efficient Market Hypothesis in the sense that we can differentiate between immediate and delayed responses in the yield difference to the program announcements. For that purpose, we estimate a distributed lag model with up to eight weekly lags.

The results of the analysis are reported in Table 13. The announcement effects for CBPP1 and CBPP2 resemble those reported in Table 11 and Table 12 in significance and direction. It is apparent that the immediate impact (at lag zero) is consistently lower than the average impacts of Table 11 and Table 12. The immediate impact of the announcement of CBPP1 on the Eurozone covered bond market is estimated at -8 bps. This compares to -12 bps in Beirne et al. (2011). The result for CBPP2 is in line with Ehlers and Sushko (2012) in that a follow-up purchase program leads to a lower effect. For CBPP3, no effect is estimated for the Eurozone.

To determine how long the announcement of the purchase programs impact yield differences, we assume that the effect ends with the first non-significant lag coefficient or with the first change in sign of the lag coefficient.[66] We note in this context that this is for interpretation purposes only, as all equations are estimated with eight lags of the announcement variable. But for ease of interpretation, Table 13 only shows those lags that we consider to be the result of the program announcements according to the above criterion.

For interpretation, it has to be noted that the fourth weekly lag coincides with the meeting of the Eurosystem's board after the initial announcement. This is also the point at which the technical details of the purchase program were announced. Lag eight represents the first period under which the outright purchases began for the three bond purchase programs.

Table 13 shows that the effect of the CBPP1 announcement lasted between four and seven weeks. This is much shorter than what is assumed by the average treatment results of Table 11 and the 56-week assumption underlying Table 12. For the second and third purchase programs, the effective duration of the announcement effect was even shorter, only between one and eight weeks.

Based on all statistically significant lag coefficients for the announcement variables in Table 13, we can find the average change in the yield spread. The results are given in Table 14. For the CBPP1 program, we find a 10-11 bps yield tightening compared to euro-denominated covered bonds issued by British banks. Only Irish covered bonds experienced a widening of 18 bps.

For CBPP2, we observe that yield spreads tighten by 4 bps for the Eurozone. This is considerably less than for the CBPP1 purchase program. A likely cause for the much lower reaction is the fact that the spreads for Germany are widening by 10 bps rather than contracting while the spreads for Spain and Ireland remain unchanged.

66 We allow for a change in sign in the first period after the announcement in CBPP2 for the Eurozone and for Ireland. We thereby find a maximum duration of the announcement effects of eight weeks.

Table 13: Unobserved Components Model with Distributed Lags

	(17) EUR	(18) GER	(19) FRA	(20) ESP	(21) IRL
OIS vs Libor Spread	0.008	0.035	0.045	-0.090	-0.132
Avg IPSI Spread	0.024***	-0.017**	-0.010*	0.077***	0.135***
iTraxx Senior Financial	0.414***	0.055	0.229	1.120***	0.564
Country$_i$ 7-3yrs IRS	-0.050	-0.349***	-0.072	-0.074	0.005
UK 7-3yrs IRS	-0.066**	-0.074	-0.054	-0.019	-0.086
CBPP1 Ann.	-0.083***	-0.111***	-0.055**	-0.073***	0.177***
CBPP1 Ann.$_{t-1}$	-0.102***	-0.124***	-0.085**	-0.115***	0.193***
CBPP1 Ann.$_{t-2}$	-0.110***	-0.122***	-0.119***	-0.115***	0.180**
CBPP1 Ann.$_{t-3}$	-0.084**	-0.101**	-0.088**	-0.083***	0.213***
CBPP1 Ann.$_{t-4}$	-0.112***	-0.094**	-0.095**	-0.120***	0.152*
CBPP1 Ann.$_{t-5}$	-0.140***	-0.128***	-0.139***	-0.155***	
CBPP1 Ann.$_{t-6}$	-0.116***	-0.121***	-0.146***	-0.096***	
CBPP1 Ann.$_{t-7}$	-0.074**	-0.098***	-0.120***	-0.040*	
CBPP1 Ann.$_{t-8}$					
CBPP2 Ann.	0.009	0.049***	0.041***	-0.003	0.051
CBPP2 Ann.$_{t-1}$	-0.032***	0.078***	-0.073***	-0.045	-0.023
CBPP2 Ann.$_{t-2}$	-0.042***	0.095***	-0.102***		
CBPP2 Ann.$_{t-3}$	-0.034**	0.122***	-0.115***		
CBPP2 Ann.$_{t-4}$	-0.062***	0.117***	-0.131***		
CBPP2 Ann.$_{t-5}$	-0.042***	0.126***	-0.134***		
CBPP2 Ann.$_{t-6}$		0.089***	-0.065***		
CBPP2 Ann.$_{t-7}$		0.108***			
CBPP2 Ann.$_{t-8}$		0.038***			
CBPP3 Ann.	-0.004	0.015***	0.013**	-0.040	-0.059***
CBPP3 Ann.$_{t-1}$	-0.006	0.043***	0.031***	-0.069*	-0.103***
CBPP3 Ann.$_{t-2}$		0.047***	0.039***		-0.080***
CBPP3 Ann.$_{t-3}$		0.034***	0.027***		-0.065**
CBPP3 Ann.$_{t-4}$		0.026***			-0.069**
CBPP3 Ann.$_{t-5}$		0.022***			-0.057**
CBPP3 Ann.$_{t-6}$		0.018**			-0.055**
CBPP3 Ann.$_{t-7}$		0.021***			
CBPP3 Ann.$_{t-8}$		0.008**			
CBPP1 Volume	0.014***	0.011***	0.009**	0.025***	0.010
CBPP2 Volume	0.021*	0.022**	0.010	0.085*	-0.063**
CBPP3 Volume	0.001	0.002	0.001	0.003	-0.001
Observations	486	486	486	486	486
Log-Likelihood	1123	986	1095	641	500
AIC	-2174	-1900	-2118	-1209	-928
BIC	-2024	-1749	-1967	-1058	-777

Estimated with an Unobserved Component Model (UCM), with the system containing a random walk component, with the variance terms not reported (the variance of the observation model is insignificant, the opposite holds true for the variance of the random walk component); missing lagged variables are omitted only for presentation purposes; the observation period is January 2, 2006 to June 26, 2015. Significance levels: * 0.10, ** 0.05, *** 0.01.

Table 14: Overview of Secondary Covered Bond Market Impacts

	Program	EUR	GER	FRA	ESP	IRL
Beirne et al. (2011)	CBPP1	-12 bps	-17 bps	-10 bps	-17 bps	not sign.
Szczerbowicz	CBPP1-2	-4 bps	-5 bps	-4 bps	-6 bps	
(2015)	CBPP1					pos.*
	CBPP2					neg.+
This Study	CBPP1	-10 bps	-11 bps	-11 bps	-11 bps	+18 bps
	CBPP2	-4 bps	+10 bps	-8 bps	not sign.	not sign.
	CBPP3	not sign.	+3 bps	+3 bps	not sign.	-7 bps

For CBPP3, there is no statistically significant announcement effect for the Eurozone as a whole. Both Germany and France show a yield spread widening of 3 bps. Only Ireland experienced a sizable and statistically significant tightening of yield spreads.

Considering the duration and size of the yield changes for all three CBPPs, the CBPP1 program clearly stands out. It led to a sizable reduction in yield spreads across all major countries and for the Eurozone in general, with only Ireland being the outlier. CBPP1 surprised the market both in its timing and its effects. As the program was conducted essentially in isolation from other policy measures, its results are the most representative for the monetary policy tool of outright covered bond purchases.

The element of surprise was not available for CBPP2. As a result, we are not able to detect as clear an impact from the announcement of CBPP2 as for CBPP1. This might possibly also be due to the market's learning that the actual purchase of covered bonds did not have much of an impact on their market pricing, leading to a lesser expectation in market movements. Only for Ireland, did actual Eurosystem purchases of covered bonds lead to a tightening in spreads (in the amount of 6 bps per €billion). This is of interest because Ireland's yield spreads exhibited the largest departure from a healthy market condition of any Eurozone country. The market reacted in the opposite direction for Spain, which experienced an increase in yield differences of 8 bps per €billion in covered bond purchases.

With regards to CBPP3, no effect can be determined for the actual bond purchases (Table 13). We observe contrary market reactions between the core countries Germany and France on the one hand and the periphery countries

Spain and Ireland on the other. That can be explained by the expectation of tightening yield spreads for the latter ones. Capital markets therefore sought additional beta exposure. They shifted their portfolios from core to periphery covered bonds and thereby increased the absolute risk in anticipation of an outperformance of periphery covered bonds. The increased yield spreads for Germany and France might be an indicator for an illiquidity premium, as investors feared a dominant market position of the Eurosystem, which reduced market liquidity.

The results of Table 11 to Table 13 are robust to a number of different specifications in terms of model specification and variable selection. We have tested for the inclusion of additional control variables, such as stock market returns and stock market volatility (e.g., Falagiarda & Reitz, 2015; Arghyrou & Kontonikas, 2012; Glick & Leduc, 2012), interbank stress, as defined by the difference between the overnight index swap and the Euribor (Szczerbowicz, 2015), and announcements of further unconventional monetary policy measures implemented by the Euroystem.

We extensively checked the results using a more conventional alternative to unobserved component modeling. In particular, we found an ARIMAX(1,1,0) model to fit well and to generate very similar results. Falagiarda and Reitz (2015), Kettemann and Krogstrup (2015), and Szczerbowicz (2015) employ similar first-difference type models. The similarity in results is not surprising given that most simple UCMs are asymptotically equivalent to an ARIMA model given certain assumptions about the error distributions. Finally, we do not find evidence for consistent market reactions based on forerunning, which is yield changes based on rumors or insider trading.

5.4 Subsidiary Conclusion

We examine the announcement effects of the three programs of covered bond purchases by the Eurosystem and their actual implementation on the yields of five European covered bond indexes. We use weekly data from January 2006 to June 2015 to cover the purchase programs of 2009/10, 2011/12, and 2014-16. We rely on a difference in difference method as our key identifying methodology. In particular, the bond yields of four countries of the Eurosystem (Germany, France, Spain, and Ireland) and the average euro-denominated bond yield are compared before and after the bond purchase announcements and before and after the actual purchases. As a basis of comparison we employ the euro-denominated covered bond yields from the United Kingdom. As UK bonds are not purchased under the Eurosystem's program, their yields can serve as our counterfactual. As a result, our analysis focuses on the bond yield difference between the Eurosystem countries and the United Kingdom.

To allow for various types of potentially unknown variables and non-stationarity, we employ an unobserved component modeling (structural time series) approach. We estimate both average effects models and distributed lag models. The latter help us to identify over how many weeks the announcement effects last.

The results are generally comparable across models, but show noteworthy differences among the three programs. The first program may be considered the most successful and the most clearly executed program, with little additional activity and market anticipation. Its announcement had a strong market impact, lowering yield spreads relative to the United Kingdom by around 10 to 11 bps, except for Ireland. These results are in line with Beirne et al. (2011).

The second purchase program did not tighten covered bond yield spreads relative to the United Kingdom. The statistical significance, the direction, and the magnitude of the effects vary among the Eurosystem countries. The third purchase program led to a tightening of spreads relative to the United Kingdom for Ireland and Spain, but to a widening for Germany and France. This inconsistency across countries makes it impossible to identify a single effect at the Eurozone level. However, is in line with capital market expectations of a relatively lower risk for the covered bonds of periphery countries.

The actual purchases of covered bonds by the Eurosystem tended to widen bond yields relative to the United Kingdom only for the first two purchase programs. This is contrary to the Eurosystem's intention for introducing the purchase programs in an aggregate volume of approximately €150 billion until mid 2015.

With the help of our distributed lag models, we can determine how long the announcement effects of the purchase programs last. We find a consistent seven week duration, except for Ireland for the first purchase program. The duration for the second and third programs cannot be generalized because it varies greatly across countries.

We conclude that the three purchase programs for covered bonds exhibit mixed effectiveness in reaching their target of improving funding conditions for banks based in the Eurozone by lowering yields and, thereby, to foster a larger credit supply. Yet the first program shows the strongest signs of reaching its goals. The two programs that follow, potentially suffer from bad market timing in the sense that they were introduced at a time when markets were healthy or capital market participants already knew the effects of outright covered bond purchases.

6 Short-term Announcement Impact on the Secondary Market[67]

In response to the GFC, the ECB undertook a number of unconventional monetary policy measures of outright asset purchases. To stabilize banks and to foster lending activity by improving the funding conditions of the financial sector, the ECB initiated three CBPPs. While it acquired €60.0 billion and €16.4 billion in covered bonds for CBPP1 and CBPP2, respectively, purchases of approximately €10 billion per month were conducted under CBPP3. As of October 2015, the Eurosystem held covered bonds totaling €163 billion, an equivalent of 29% of all bonds eligible under either CBPP (Beaumont, 2015). As the ECB initiated CBPP2 and CBPP 3, their goal description became increasingly functional (Appendix 1); however, it can be assumed that all three programs translate into the goal of a liquid market for covered bonds, trading at tight spreads.

For sovereign bonds, many authors find the announcements of unconventional monetary policy measures led to a tightening of spreads (Falagiarda & Reitz, 2015; Watfe, 2015; Rivolta, 2014; Kilponen et al., 2015).[68] When differentiating between European countries, the unconventional monetary policy literature finds very different results in the covered and sovereign bond markets (Beirne et al., 2011; Szczerbowicz, 2015; Faliagarda & Reitz, 2015; Altavilla et al., 2016; Rivolta, 2014), since each country exhibited different levels of stress during the sovereign debt crisis. Gibson et al. (2016) and Eser and Schwab (2016) document that the effectiveness of the programs varies with the remaining time to maturity.

Only few authors focus on the announcement effects of unconventional monetary policy measures in the covered bond market. They find similar results as for the sovereign bond market, in that yields tend to tighten. Kettemann and Krogstrup (2013) find a similar result for Swiss covered bond purchases. While

---

67 This Section is co-authored by Ferdinand Mager, Jan Mutl, and Nico B. Rottke.

68 See also Gagnon, Raskin, Remache, and Sack (2011), and Krishnamurthy and Vissing-Jorgensen (2011) for the United States; Joyce, Lasaosa, Stevens, and Tong (2011) for the United Kingdom; and Bernoth and Erdogan (2012), Falagiarda and Reitz (2015), Neely (2015), and Pattipeilohy et al. (2013) for the eurozone.

H. Markmann, *Covered Bonds under Unconventional Monetary Policy*,
Essays in Real Estate Research 14,
https://doi.org/10.1007/978-3-658-20975-9_6

Beirne et al. (2011) cannot detect a significant effect of outright covered bond purchases[69] on yields, Gibson et al. (2016) confirm an additional tightening effect.

Our study builds on two strands of literature, on covered bond pricing and unconventional monetary policy, to which we make several contributions. First, our study includes the more recent purchase programs. Second, our comprehensive dataset allows our analyses to include bond-specific characteristics, such as maturity, rating, and country of origin. Third, we include announcements of CBPP technical details and other outright bond purchase programs—the SMP, OMT, and the PSPP—in our empirical analysis. Finally, since our dataset extends to covered bonds of non-eurozone members that are not (directly) subject to the ECB policy, we have a natural control group. This allows us to employ a difference-in-difference approach and thereby improve the ability to infer causality compared to previous studies.

At 3% for individual covered bonds, we find CBPP1 to have been less effective in tightening covered bond spreads than suggested by Beirne et al. (2011) and in line with Szczerbowicz (2015) in terms of index levels. For CBPP2 and CBPP3, we do not observe a general tightening of covered bond spreads. However, for the announcement of sovereign bond purchase programs, we find evidence of the ECB achieving its goals of suppressing covered bond yields for stressed countries on a short-term basis. We conclude the covered bond market responds slowly but efficiently to unexpected unconventional monetary policy announcements when there is a clear rationale for central bank intervention.

The remainder of this Section is organized as follows: Sub-section 2 briefly summarizes the unconventional monetary policy instruments employed by the ECB, the literature on covered bond pricing, and the literature on unconventional monetary policy. Sub-section 3 describes our dataset and methodology. Sub-section 4 presents our results, before Sub-section 5 concludes the Section.

6.1 Literature

Due to their dual recourse structure, covered bonds traditionally trade at very low spreads to sovereign bonds.[70] During the pre-crisis period, credit risk was not a

---

[69] That is, open market purchases rather than the announcement thereof.

main concern, as confirmed, for example, by Breger and Stovel (2004), who cannot find an effect of individual bond ratings. Prokopczuk and Vonhoff (2012) show that, since the onset of the GFC in mid-2007, the quality of the underlying pool of mortgages has had an impact on the pricing of covered bonds. Kempf et al. (2012), Prokopczuk and Vonhoff (2012), and Prokopczuk, Siewert, and Vonhoff (2013) find that credit risk is reflected in bond ratings. The literature generally agrees on liquidity being a major driver of differences in covered bond pricing (Buchholst et al., 2010; Siewert & Vonhoff, 2011).

Following the examples of the U.S. Federal Reserve, the Bank of England, and the Bank of Japan, in 2009, the ECB (2009, p. 18) prepared the market for the introduction of unconventional monetary policy instruments to mitigate "exceptional market conditions." These measures included direct liquidity injections and asset purchases, as well as the subsequent forward-looking policy statements. With difficult funding conditions in capital markets, unconventional monetary policy interventions became largely viable and expected in the following months. Nonetheless, the announcement of the ECB's first asset purchase program, namely, CBPP1, was largely surprising in its scope (Beirne et al., 2011; Szczerbowicz, 2015). Via direct purchases of covered bonds in primary and secondary markets, the ECB (2009) aimed to foster a decline in money market term rates, easing funding conditions for banks, to improve debt market liquidity. The first program was announced in May 2009, with its technical details specified four weeks later. The actual purchases under the program ran for a 12-month period starting in July 2009 and targeted euro-denominated covered bonds, issued under eurozone covered bond legislation,[71] with a minimum outstanding volume of €500 million,[72] a remaining maturity of three to seven years, and at least an AA rating. To qualify for purchases, the bonds also had to be UCITS compliant or similarly structured to be eligible for ECB repo transactions (ECB, 2009; Packmohr & Weigerding, 2015). By June 2010, the Eurosystem had purchased covered bonds up to the targeted total acquisition costs of €60 billion, of which 27% were purchased in primary markets and 73% in secondary markets

[70] Covered bonds can be benchmarked against either the asset swap or the respective sovereign bond yield. While the latter is not as common, sell-side institutions only refer to the asset swap spread. The statement also holds for swap spreads. In both cases, spreads can turn negative.

[71] 'Structured covered bonds', particularly common in France, were excluded.

[72] In exceptional cases, €100 million

(ECB, 2010). Table 15 provides an overview of all ECB unconventional monetary policy announcements with respect to outright asset purchases until February 2015.

Table 15: Announcement Dates of the Eurosystem's Asset Purchase Programs

Event	Date	Description
CBPP1 Announcement	May 07, 2009	Eurosystem announces its decision to purchase covered bonds (CBPP1) and a 12M LTRO facility
CBPP1 Technical Details	Jun 04, 2009	Technical annex for CBPP1, including €60 billion target and eligibility, is announced
SMP Announcement	May 10, 2010	Eurosystem announces its decision to purchase private and sovereign debt, focusing on sovereign debt from Greece, Ireland, and Portugal
SMP Reactivation	Aug 07, 2011	Eurosystem announces its decision to resume the SMP to acquire sovereign debt from Italy and Spain
CBPP2 Announcement	Oct 06, 2011	Eurosystem announces its decision to purchase covered bonds (CBPP2)
CBPP2 Technical Details	Nov 03, 2011	Technical annex for CBPP2, including €40 billion target and eligibility, is announced
Draghi: "Whatever it takes"	Jun 06, 2012	Mario Draghi delivers a speech indicating to undertake all measures required to safeguard the Eurozone
OMT Indication	Aug 02, 2012	Eurosystem announces its intention to implement an outright purchase program
OMT Announcement	Sep 06, 2012	Eurosystem announces its decision to implement a program allowing for sovereign bond purchases to replace the SMP
CBPP3 Announcement	Sep 04, 2014	Eurosystem announces its decision to purchase covered bonds (CBPP3) and Asset Backed Securities (ABSPP)
CBPP3 Technical Details	Oct 02, 2014	Technical annex for CBPP3, including eligibility but excluding volume, is announced
PSPP Announcement	Jan 22, 2015	Eurosystem announces its decision to purchase sovereign bonds (PSPP)

At the height of the sovereign debt crisis in early May 2010, the ECB launched the SMP to purchase private and public debt instruments. It largely targeted Greek, Irish, and Portuguese sovereign bond markets, which had become dysfunctional. After a period of improved market conditions, the Italian and Spanish sovereign bond markets began to be severely affected by the sovereign debt crisis and the ECB announced the reactivation of the SMP in July 2011 to purchase the sovereign bonds of these two countries (Eser et al. 2012).

Along the lines of CBPP1, a second program was announced in October 2011 that was aimed at purchasing €40 billion in covered bonds. Unlike for the first program, the announcement was anticipated by the capital markets. Again, the program was scheduled to last 12 months and to be active in the primary and secondary markets. However, the requirements for covered bonds to be eligible under the program were relaxed. In particular, the minimum volume outstanding was reduced to €300 million, the rating requirement was lowered to investment grade, and the maximum maturity extended to 10.5 years (ECB, 2011). The program did not match the ECB's expectations, since only €16 billion in covered bond were purchased, 37% of which was in the primary market and 63% in the secondary market.

On June 26, 2012, as the sovereign debt crisis was reaching new levels of anxiety, ECB president Mario Draghi delivered a speech at a London conference in which he stated, "Within our mandate, the ECB is ready to do whatever it takes to preserve the euro. And believe me, it will be enough" (ECB, 2012). While this statement was not aimed at the covered bond market, it largely impacted markets, since it underlined the ECB's intention to (potentially) implement further unconventional monetary policy measures. The following week, Draghi affirmed his statement by specifying that the Eurosystem could engage in outright purchase programs. Finally, in September 2012, the OMT was established to acquire sovereign debt with maturities between one and three years in secondary markets. To date, the OMT has not been activated but only been added to the ECB's toolbox (Eser, Amaro, Iacobelli, & Rubens, 2012; Altavilla et al., 2016).

In the fall of 2014, the covered bond market was in sound condition and exhibited spreads significantly below crisis levels when the ECB announced a third CBPP. However, while the goals remained largely unchanged, the rationale did not. The purchases now aimed at injecting liquidity into the markets instead of improving deteriorated funding conditions. As such, the ABSPP was announced at the same time. Both programs were scheduled to run for 24 months and account for a purchase volume of approximately €10 billion per month, of which the latter program only contributes a fraction (ECB, 2016). The purchase requirements were eased again, in that Cypriot and Greek covered bonds became eligible up to 30% of the outstanding volume, volume and maturity restrictions were lifted, and fully retained issues became explicitly eligible. On the contrary, the Eurosystem limited aggregate purchases of covered bonds under its three programs to 70% of the outstanding amount of each bond issue (ECB, 2014).

While capital market participants expected the implementation of some monetary policy measure to inject liquidity, the inclusion of covered bonds came as a surprise, particularly considering the success of CBPP2, the state of covered bond markets, and the large portion of eligible assets already held by the Eurosystem. With the realization of the actual purchase volumes, fears of the ECB taking a dominant role in the covered bond market were substantial (Beaumont, 2015). As of September 2016, a total of €194.3 billion in covered bonds were held by the Eurosystem and the share of primary market purchases under CBPP3 amounted to 29% (ECB, 2016). [73] Finally, in February 2015, the ECB announced the PSPP, an extension of CBPP3 and the ABSPP in terms of acquiring sovereign debt on the secondary market.

Academic research on unconventional monetary policy is mainly focused on sovereign bonds.[74] Further areas of research with respect to unconventional monetary policy include exchange rates (Neely, 2015), credit default swaps (Alter & Beyer, 2014), and macroeconomic measures (Lenza, Pill, & Reichlin, 2010; Altavilla et al., 2016; Kucharčuková, Claeys, & Vašíček, 2014).

Research on the impact of unconventional monetary policy on the covered bond market is still rather limited. We are aware of four papers that focus on this market segment. Beirne et al. (2011) analyze the effects of CBPP1 on primary and secondary covered bond markets. They find a significant tightening of covered bond yields, a reduction in short-term financing rates, increased primary covered bond issuance activity, and increased market liquidity. Their secondary market analysis aims to identify level changes for several covered bond indexes upon the announcement of CBPP1. They identify a tightening of 12 bps for all

---

[73] At amortized costs and subject to end-of-quarter-adjustments and maturing bonds.

[74] For example, Gagnon et al. (2011), and Krishnamurthy and Vissing-Jorgensen (2011) for the United States, Joyce et al. (2011) for the United Kingdom, and Bernoth and Erdogan (2012), Falagiarda and Reitz (2015), Neely (2015), and Pattipeilohy et al. (2013) for the eurozone.

euro-denominated covered bonds and 17 bps, 10 bps, and 17 bps for the German, French, and Spanish covered bond indexes, respectively. The authors fail to find a significant effect for the Irish covered bond index. Contrary to the announcement, Beirne et al. do not report an impact of actual covered bond purchases.

In a broader study, Szczerbowicz (2015) reports a long-term tightening of covered bond yield spreads versus German Bunds of 4 bps after the announcements of CBPP1 and CBPP2. The author's study also employs covered bond indexes and treats the announcements of the two programs as equivalent, ruling out differentiation between the two. The author's country-specific results show only minor differences for Germany, France, and Spain.

Gibson et al. (2016) find evidence of a cumulative increase in covered bond prices of up to 15% due to the implementation of CBPP1. Their analysis for the covered bond indexes from Greece, Ireland, Italy, Portugal, and Spain is based on monthly time series data.

Kettemann and Krogstrup (2013) analyze the Swiss National Bank's covered bond purchase program, which was announced in March 2009 and extended until September of the same year. They report a 10-bp tightening of covered bond spreads versus Swiss sovereign bonds. Since the duration and volume of the program were not communicated at the time of the announcement, the full effect of the announcement unfolded during the course of the next couple of trading days. Subsequently, the Swiss National Bank disposed of its covered bond holdings to the open market in 2010 and the authors are not able to determine an impact of this undertaking on covered bond spreads.

While numerous studies consider the effect of CBPPs on sovereign bond yields (e.g., Watfe, 2015), only Szczerbowicz (2015) considers the effect of sovereign bond programs on covered bond yields. Interestingly, the author finds that, upon the announcement of sovereign bond purchase programs, covered bond yields react more strongly than upon the announcement of CBPPs.[75]

We hypothesize that ECB announcements of unconventional monetary policy measures (that came as a surprise) led to an immediate tightening of spreads,

[75] We do not further investigate the potential cause in a reaction to movements of the German Bund, which serves as Szczerbowicz's (2015) normalizing variable. As a reference, Altavilla, Giannone, and Lenza (2014) do not find significant changes of the German Bund upon OMT announcements; however, their magnitude is in the range of the results observed by Szczerbowicz (2015).

with more pronounced effects for longer maturities. We further expect to see larger effects for covered bonds from periphery countries that experienced more deteriorating capital market conditions during the crisis.

6.2 Data and Methodology

We use a dataset of 1,130 euro-denominated covered bonds that constitute the Markit iBoxx EUR Covered index from June 2008 to June 2015.[76] Our sample covers bonds from the core countries of Austria, France, Germany, and the Netherlands (accounting for a total of $n = 604$ bonds), as well as the periphery countries (Falagiarda & Reitz, 2015) of Ireland, Italy,[77] Portugal, and Spain ($n = 333$). We consider only bonds with a time to maturity of one year to 10 years. Bonds from Canada, Norway, Sweden, the United Kingdom, and the United States ($n = 193$) serve as a control sample, since they are not eligible under the Eurosystem's purchase programs.

While the bond ratings were obtained from Markit, all remaining data were obtained from Thomson Reuters (Datastream and Eikon). Table 16 shows descriptive statistics with panel A depicting the ratings across countries. As expected, most bonds are rated AAA (68%) or AA (17%). We see the majority of A or BBB ratings from Spain and Italy, in addition to Ireland and Portugal, we classify as periphery countries (e.g., Falagiarda & Reitz, 2015). We identify no rating below investment grade and maturities across countries seem to be well balanced, with an average of 4.3 years.[78]

76 To be included in the index, bonds must fulfill a number of criteria, such as classification under article 52 of UCITS (fixed rate bonds with cash flows known at issuance, with a volume of at least €500 million). Our sample for covered bonds from the eurozone-area thereby largely fulfills the ECB's eligibility criteria. We assume all bonds part of Markit's iBoxx index to be eligible for covered bond purchases. We test for the relaxation of this assumption by generating an eligibility list based on the detailed eligibility criteria published by the ECB based on maturity, legal status, rating, and the ECB's list of eligible assets for the purpose of repo transactions. This analysis leads to consistent results, with slightly larger coefficients. French structured covered bonds are not "issued pursuant to legislation governing covered bonds that is in force in a euro area member State" (ECB, 2009, p. 19) and are therefore not eligible for purchases under either CBPP. The results of a specific analysis mimic those of the eurozone and are therefore not expected to introduce a bias.

77 Only as of January 2009, since the iBoxx index for Italy was only released in January of the same year.

78 Only France exhibits a relatively higher larger proportion of bonds in the seven- to 10-year bracket.

Table 16: Number of Covered Bond Yield Swap Spread Observations

	Core				Periphery					
	AUT	**FRA**	**GER**	**NED**	**ESP**	**IRL**	**ITA**	**POR**	**Controls**	**Total**
Total:	26,136	181,777	187,097	34,842	189,185	19,902	40,693	15,967	145,492	84,1091
Panel A: By Rating										
AAA	17,991	161,448	129,258	29,335	80,695	5,083	8,637	5,111	132,184	569,742
AA	8,145	20,329	53,069	5,507	25,610	4,559	7,674	2,752	11,474	139,119
A	0	0	4,684	0	54,387	7,299	18,967	1,073	1,834	88,244
BBB	0	0	86	0	28,493	2,961	5,415	7,031	0	43,986
Panel B: By Maturity										
1-3 Years	8,379	51,749	88,467	7,545	71,785	7,786	11,532	6,293	50,563	304,099
3-7 Years	13,379	84,418	83,076	17,605	88,660	10,472	22,367	8,074	75,634	403,685
7-10 Years	4,378	45,610	15,554	9,692	28,740	1,644	6,794	1,600	19,295	133,307
Panel C: By Announcement Date										
CBPP1 Ann.	7	64	114	9	94	10	4	8	50	360
CBPP1 Details Ann.	7	65	113	10	90	11	4	8	51	359
SMP Ann.	6	78	101	15	105	12	9	14	64	404
SMP Reactivation	7	106	95	20	122	11	22	10	82	475
CBPP2 Ann.	7	109	89	21	119	11	22	10	85	473
CBPP2 Details Ann.	7	106	88	21	118	11	23	10	86	470
Draghi Statement	23	113	102	21	122	8	29	9	98	525
OMT Indication	23	115	108	21	124	8	31	9	98	537
OMT Ann.	21	115	107	23	124	8	32	9	99	538
CBPP3 Ann.	23	122	103	26	85	12	42	6	99	518
CBPP3 Details Ann.	24	123	103	25	82	12	41	6	99	515
PSPP Ann.	24	121	101	24	76	10	40	6	104	506

Each observation in Panel C represents one bond, i.e. the number of observations for the [0,0]-day event window.

While the majority of the previous literature has analyzed covered bonds with reference to sovereign bonds, we use the asset swap rate as appropriate benchmark. Whereas the asset swap captures general fluctuations in the money market, the spread measures the credit and liquidity risk of an individual bond. We consider government risk as a substantial element of credit risk. To capture announcement effects, we construct a covered bond yield spread variable over the asset swap rate with an equivalent remaining time to maturity[79] that serves as the dependent variable of our analysis. Figure 15 depicts the mean and quartile swap spread development for our sample period. Before the GFC, swap spreads reflected only a slight liquidity premium, while credit risk was largely ignored. Starting in 2009Q3, we see an increasing discrimination for credit risk in covered bond pricing. From 2013Q3 onward, we observe a decrease in credit spreads leading to a narrower band of covered bond yields.

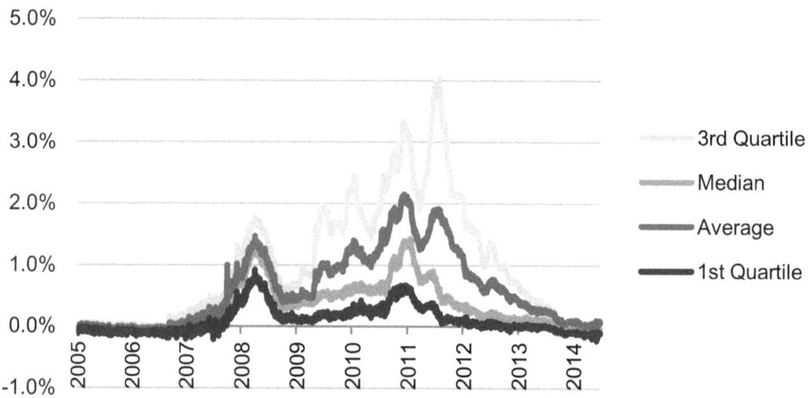

Figure 15: Covered Bond Swap Spreads
Quartile and average bid-ask-spreads of covered bonds included in Markit iBoxx euro-denominated covered bond index. The bid-ask-spread is defined as the proportional difference between the bid price and the ask price in relation to the ask price. Year marks represent the year end. Source: Own Illustration based on Datastream

[79] Methodologically in line with Durbin and Ng (2005)

We use several control variables. The remaining time to maturity of each covered bond, *Time to Maturity,* controls for yield changes along the interest structure. To proxy for differences in the quality of the cover pool, as suggested by Prokopczuk and Vonhoff (2012), we use the issuer's rating (*Rating Dummies*) provided by Markit, as employed by Prokopczuk et al. (2013).[80]

Further, we employ the sovereign yield spread versus the Germany Bund (maturity matched), *Sovereign vs. Germany*, as a proxy for country credit risk, since country credit risk greatly varied during the GFC (Szczerbowicz, 2015). We thereby abstain from including a specific GFC proxy variable, such as volatility indexes (e.g., Falagiarda & Reitz, 2015; Glick & Leduc, 2012). Instead, we include dummy variables to capture the covered bond's country of origination and type, *Country and Sector Dummy*, respectively, where appropriate.[81] These measures account for differing legislatures and tax treatments, found to be relevant by Volk and Hillenbrand (2006). Due to lacking data frequency, we do not include housing market data, as previously done by Prokopczuk and Vonhoff (2012). In addition, as our final credit risk variable, we employ the *Banking Sector Risk* variable, defined as the difference between the yield of the iBoxx euro-denominated bank subordinated debt and the respective index of senior bank debt, similar to Kempf et al. (2012). This measure proxies for the risk of the banking sector in general and its ability to attract wholesale funding. To control for liquidity effects, we employ a proportional bid–ask-spread, *Bid-Ask-Spread*, as our measure for trading liquidity (Prokopczuk & Vonhoff, 2012; Delatte, Fouquau, & Portes, 2016). Finally, we include a time dummy, *Individual Quarter Dummy*, at the quarter level to account for market behavior in a broad sense. Since all the bonds in our sample are denominated in euros, issuers and investors not reporting in euros are subject to currency translation. To correct for potential investor currency mismatching, we employ as a further variable the cross-currency swap spread of the matching maturity, *FX SWAP equiv.,* as a control variable, drawing from Beirne et al. (2011).[82]

---

80 Ratings do not exhibit any value worse than investment grade and represent an aggregated average of Standard & Poor's, Fitch, and Moody's, without a consideration of notching. Rating agency methodology is inherently subject to a sovereign rating ceiling.

81 This is the case for German mortgage and public covered bonds; French structured, legal, and Société de Financement de l'Habitat covered bonds; and Spanish single and multi cédulas.

82 For eurozone countries, this variable naturally takes the value of zero.

Previous literature on the announcement effects of unconventional monetary policy relies on different methods, such as first differences and autoregressive models (Faliagarda & Reitz, 2015; Watfe 2015; Szczerbowicz, 2015; Christensen & Gillan, 2016). Wafte (2015) uses a GARCH model and Beirne et al. (2011) employ a pooled ordinary least squares model. Our methodology is similar to that of Rees (2001), Prokopczuk and Vonhoff (2012), and Prokopczuk, Siewert, and Vonhoff (2013) with regard to the model setup. We use a pricing model on the basis of individual bonds, which takes the form

$$CB\ Yield_{i,t} - SWAP_{i,t} = \alpha_i + \beta_1^{'} X_{i,t} + \mu_t + \epsilon_{i,t} \tag{10}$$

$$\epsilon_{i,t} = \rho * \epsilon_{i,t-1} + \eta_{i,t} \tag{11}$$

where the dependent variable $CB\ Yield_{i,t} - SWAP_{i,t}$ represents the covered bond spread versus the asset swap of a matching maturity and $\boldsymbol{X_{i,t}}$ represents a vector of control variables (Table 17). As described earlier, $\boldsymbol{X_{i,t}}$ contains the *Time to Maturity* of the individual covered bonds, their *Bid-Ask-Spread*, and *Rating Dummies* as bond-specific measures. The credit risk at the country level is included via the *Sovereign vs. Germany* spread and the floating rate *FX SWAP equiv.* This is supplemented with the risk measure of *Banking Sector Risk.* The vector also includes *Country & Sector Dummies* and *Individual Quarter Dummies* and $\mu_{i,t}$ accounts for random effects.[83] We use generalized least squares and autocorrelation corrected standard errors of degree one (see Eq. 12).[84]

Table 17: Descriptive Statistics of Independent Variables

	N	Range	Percentile			Mean	Std. Dev.
			5th	Median	95th		
Time to Maturity	841,091	9.0	1.27	3.90	9.00	4.34	2.371
Bid-Ask-Spread	841,091	0.2	0.00	0.00	0.02	0.01	0.006
Sovereign vs. Germany	841,091	28.7	0.00	0.34	3.52	0.89	1.454
FX SWAP equiv.	841,091	144.1	0.00	0.00	22.99	2.80	8.767
Banking Sector Risk	841,091	9.4	0.90	2.16	5.72	2.69	1.689

Similar to Eser and Schwab (2016), we employ a difference-in-difference estimator that assumes that the control group provides counterfactual behavior to

---

[83] The Breusch–Pagan Lagrange multiplier test rejects the null hypothesis that the variance of random effects is zero.

[84] The Wooldridge test for first-order autocorrelation is rejected at the 5% level.

that of the eurozone if the Eurosystem had abstained from implementing its intervention measures. That is, covered bonds in different countries co-move under normal market conditions, so that they follow a parallel path.

For our event study design, we need to assume that the ECB announcements came as a surprise to the market, which we confirm via popular press analysis through the Nexis database. However, this is not the case for CBPP2, since its announcement was largely anticipated. The same holds true for the announcements of the OMT programs and the technical details of CBPPs taking place at the ECB governing council meeting subsequent to the initial program announcement. Similar to Watfe (2015), we analyze 12 ECB announcements of unconventional monetary policy measures (see Table 15).

We employ four event windows ([-5;-1], [-2,2], [0,0], and [1,5]), in line with previous research on ECB announcement effects.[85] In our discussion we will manly focus on the [2,2]-day event window, as it is sufficiently long to capture the announcement effect.

Our final regression therefore takes the following form:

$$CB\ Yield_{i,t} - SWAP_{i,t} =$$
$$\alpha_i + \beta_1' X_{i,t} + \beta_2 \sum_{k=1}^{8} Ann[p,q]_{k,t} + \beta_3 Eurozone \times \sum_{k=1}^{8} Ann[p,q]_{k,t} +$$
$$\mu_t + \epsilon_{i,t} \qquad (12)$$

$$\epsilon_{i,t} = \rho * \epsilon_{i,t-1} + \eta_{i,t} \qquad (13)$$

where $Ann[p,q]_{k,t}$ is a set of eight variables for $k = \{1, ..., 8\}$ that take the value of one if within the interval of [p,q] trading days around the announcement of an unconventional monetary policy measure and zero otherwise. The regression also includes a eurozone dummy that separates eligible bonds (issued in the eurozone) and non-eligible bonds.[86] The interaction term $Eurozone \times Ann[p,q]_{k,t}$ captures the spread change that can be attributed solely to the ECB's announcements and which is therefore unique to covered bonds eligible under the CBPPs.

[85] The literature on sovereign bond and equity markets (e.g., Falagiarda & Reitz, 2015; Neely, 2015; Christensen & Gillan, 2016; Joyce et al., 2011; Ricci, 2014) considers event windows of up to four days. Alter and Beyer (2014) even use a considerably larger event window of [-10,10] days for the credit default swap market. For the covered bond market, Szczerbowicz (2015) employs a [0,0]-day event window.

[86] The eurozone dummy is not explicitly shown in the output, since it is a collinear combination of Country & Sector Dummies.

6.3 Results

Table 18 provides the results for our regression analysis of the whole sample. As expected, longer maturities (*Time to Maturity*) lead to a larger spread and illiquidity (*Bid-Ask-Spread*) comes at the cost of a wider swap spread. The same holds true for the general risk premium as proxied by the sovereign yield versus the German Bund yield (*Sovereign vs. Germany*). Similarly, a larger *Banking Sector Risk* is associated with generally larger risk premia for covered bonds.

With respect to the announcement effects of the ECB's unconventional monetary policy measures, we find mixed effects for the swap spread. These results only partly confirm the findings of Beirne et al. (2011) and Szczerbowicz (2015).

For unconventional monetary policy announcements directly aimed at the covered bond market,[87] we observe a 3-bp spread tightening for the announcement of CBPP1 in the [-2,2]-day event window. For the core countries (Table 19), we see a tightening of covered bonds spreads of approximately 4 bps for the same announcement. This is generally in line with the findings of Beirne et al. (2011) and Szczerbowicz (2015). Additionally, we note a 3-bp anticipation effect. Interestingly, the announcement day itself does not yield significant results.

In our detailed country analysis (Table 20), we note that Dutch covered bonds do not show any significant reaction to the ECB's announcement of CBPP1, while the above-mentioned spread tightening can largely be attributed to the very liquid German market, with a tightening of 5 bps.

For the periphery countries, the announcement of CBPP1 led to a similar overall spread tightening of 3 bps in the [-2,2]-day event window; however, the markets reacted in a more volatile manner, since the change for the actual announcement day was positive, at 5 bps. Taking into account the individual country effects of Table 21, the result holds for Spain, but the same cannot be confirmed for the other countries at the 10% significance level. We observe a 12-bp widening for Irish covered bonds. These results for the periphery countries do not support the findings of Beirne et al. (2011) and Szczerbowicz (2015); neither does it confirm Falagiarda and Reitz's (2016) and Altavilla et al.'s (2016) finding of stronger tightening in periphery countries when analyzing the effects of SMP and OMT announcements in sovereign markets.

---

[87] That is, CBPP1 to CBPP3 and the announcements of the respective technical details.

Table 18: Regression Results for All Countries

	(22) [-5,-1]	(23) [-2,2]	(24) [0,0]	(25) [1,5]
Time to Maturity	0.050***	0.050***	0.050***	0.050***
Bid-Ask-Spread	2.146***	2.143***	2.187***	2.165***
Sovereign vs. Germany	0.121***	0.122***	0.121***	0.122***
Banking Sector Risk	0.078***	0.071***	0.071***	0.071***
FX SWAP equiv.	-0.001***	-0.001***	-0.001***	-0.001***
CBPP1 Ann. [p,q]	-0.008	0.015	0.048***	-0.035**
CBPP1 Details Ann. [p,q]	-0.050***	-0.010	0.031**	0.007
SMP Ann. [p,q]	0.019	-0.004	-0.028**	0.036***
SMP Reactivation [p,q]	0.035***	-0.158***	-0.107***	0.036***
CBPP2 Ann. [p,q]	-0.033***	-0.015	0.071***	-0.072***
CBPP2 Details Ann. [p,q]	0.106***	0.021*	-0.035***	-0.025**
Draghi Statement [p,q]	0.017	-0.038***	0.017	-0.028**
OMT Indication [p,q]	0.052***	-0.045***	-0.077***	0.043***
OMT Ann. [p,q]	-0.039***	-0.023**	0.037***	-0.066***
CBPP3 Ann. [p,q]	0.021**	0.003	-0.039***	0.012
CBPP3 Details Ann. [p,q]	-0.016	-0.010	0.014	-0.002
PSPP Ann. [p,q]	0.023**	0.015	-0.038***	0.015
Eurozone × CBPP1 Ann. [p,q]	-0.008	-0.027*	0.016	-0.013
Eurozone × CBPP1 Details Ann. [p,q]	0.003	0.002	-0.007	0.017
Eurozone × SMP Ann. [p,q]	0.034**	0.012	-0.026*	-0.012
Eurozone × SMP Reactivation [p,q]	-0.004	0.001	-0.000	0.007
Eurozone × CBPP2 Ann. [p,q]	0.003	0.007	0.000	0.007
Eurozone × CBPP2 Details Ann. [p,q]	-0.005	-0.021*	-0.003	0.000
Eurozone × Draghi Statement [p,q]	0.012	0.015	0.005	0.026**
Eurozone × OMT Indication [p,q]	0.024*	0.012	0.005	0.019
Eurozone × OMT Ann. [p,q]	0.009	0.008	0.008	0.004
Eurozone × CBPP3 Ann. [p,q]	-0.001	0.003	0.012	-0.013
Eurozone × CBPP3 Details Ann. [p,q]	0.002	0.005	0.002	-0.002
Eurozone × PSPP Ann. [p,q]	0.000	0.001	0.001	0.001
Rating Dummy	yes	yes	yes	yes
Country & Sector Dummy	yes	yes	yes	yes
Individual Quarter Dummy	yes	yes	yes	yes
Constant	-0.343***	-0.313***	-0.317***	-0.316***
Observations	841091	841091	841091	841091
Groups	1130	1130	1130	1130
R^2	0.635	0.634	0.633	0.635
Rho AR	0.978	0.978	0.978	0.978

The regression results show the impact on individual covered bonds' yield spread versus the asset swap with an equivalent maturity, which serves as the independent variable. Regressions (22) through (25) vary in the event windows [p,q] considered for the analysis of announcement effects. The sample period is from June 12, 2008, to June 30, 2015. Significance levels: * 0.10, ** 0.05, *** 0.01.

Table 19: Regression Results for Core/Periphery Countries

	(26) [-5,-1]	(27) [-2,2]	(28) [0,0]	(29) [1,5]
Core Countries				
Eurozone × CBPP1 Ann. [p,q]	-0.031*	-0.042**	-0.009	-0.040**
Eurozone × CBPP1 Details Ann. [p,q]	-0.057***	-0.031*	-0.023	-0.032*
Eurozone × SMP Ann. [p,q]	-0.012	-0.012	0.017	-0.008
Eurozone × SMP Reactivation [p,q]	-0.005	-0.008	-0.001	-0.004
Eurozone × CBPP2 Ann. [p,q]	0.008	0.015	0.002	0.016
Eurozone × CBPP2 Details Ann. [p,q]	-0.003	-0.065***	-0.008	0.006
Eurozone × Draghi Statement [p,q]	0.018	0.012	-0.002	0.024
Eurozone × OMT Indication [p,q]	0.026*	0.015	-0.008	0.026*
Eurozone × OMT Ann. [p,q]	0.010	0.014	0.002	0.012
Eurozone × CBPP3 Ann. [p,q]	0.007	0.012	0.014	0.002
Eurozone × CBPP3 Details Ann. [p,q]	0.005	0.012	0.006	0.010
Eurozone × PSPP Ann. [p,q]	-0.007	0.007	0.002	-0.003
Periphery Countries				
Eurozone × CBPP1 Ann. [p,q]	-0.013	-0.028*	0.045***	-0.032**
Eurozone × CBPP1 Details Ann. [p,q]	0.005	0.003	-0.011	0.025
Eurozone × SMP Ann. [p,q]	0.108***	0.042***	-0.087***	-0.022
Eurozone × SMP Reactivation [p,q]	0.008	0.001	-0.017	0.014
Eurozone × CBPP2 Ann. [p,q]	0.005	0.003	-0.003	0.002
Eurozone × CBPP2 Details Ann. [p,q]	-0.013	-0.026**	0.003	-0.003
Eurozone × Draghi Statement [p,q]	0.033**	0.043***	0.009	0.048***
Eurozone × OMT Indication [p,q]	0.036**	0.033**	0.026**	0.023*
Eurozone × OMT Ann. [p,q]	0.025**	0.011	0.018	0.002
Eurozone × CBPP3 Ann. [p,q]	0.013	0.005	0.007	-0.024*
Eurozone × CBPP3 Details Ann. [p,q]	0.010	0.006	0.004	-0.012
Eurozone × PSPP Ann. [p,q]	0.002	-0.004	0.003	-0.003

The regression results show the impact on individual covered bonds' yield spread versus the asset swap with an equivalent maturity, which serves as the independent variable. Regressions (26) through (29) vary in the event windows [p,q] considered for the analysis of announcement effects. The sample period is from June 12, 2008, to June 30, 2015. The controls variables Time to Maturity, Bid-Ask-Spread, Sovereign vs. Germany, Banking Sector Risk, and FX SWAP equiv.; the overall day effects for CBPP1 to CBPP3 and their technical detail announcements; the SMP and its reactivation; and the OMT announcements are omitted for ease of reading. The same holds true for Rating Dummies, Country & Sector Dummies, and the Individual Quarter Dummies. The regressions comprise of 797 covered bonds (R^2 = 52.7 to 52.9%) for the core countries and 526 (R^2 = 50.9 to 51.3%) for the periphery countries. Significance levels: * 0.10, ** 0.05, *** 0.01.

Table 20: Individual Country Regression Results for Core Countries

	(30) **[-5,-1]**	(31) **[-2,2]**	(32) **[0,0]**	(33) **[1,5]**
Austria				
Eurozone × CBPP1 Ann. [p,q]	-0.021	-0.018	-0.006	0.004
Eurozone × CBPP1 Details Ann. [p,q]	-0.013	-0.005	-0.006	-0.009
Eurozone × SMP Ann. [p,q]	0.015	0.006	0.004	0.006
Eurozone × SMP Reactivation [p,q]	-0.013	-0.006	-0.005	-0.004
Eurozone × CBPP2 Ann. [p,q]	-0.006	-0.012	-0.002	-0.009
Eurozone × CBPP2 Details Ann. [p,q]	-0.011	-0.111**	-0.003	-0.010
Eurozone × Draghi Statement [p,q]	0.003	0.014	-0.009	0.016
Eurozone × OMT Indication [p,q]	-0.010	0.022	0.021	-0.003
Eurozone × OMT Ann. [p,q]	0.010	0.005	-0.008	0.013
Eurozone × CBPP3 Ann. [p,q]	-0.002	0.005	0.012	-0.006
Eurozone × CBPP3 Details Ann. [p,q]	-0.005	-0.000	0.007	-0.003
Eurozone × PSPP Ann. [p,q]	-0.009	0.010	0.001	-0.009
France				
Eurozone × CBPP1 Ann. [p,q]	-0.005	-0.034*	0.015	-0.029
Eurozone × CBPP1 Details Ann. [p,q]	-0.021	-0.006	-0.015	0.002
Eurozone × SMP Ann. [p,q]	-0.016	-0.011	0.018	-0.008
Eurozone × SMP Reactivation [p,q]	0.002	-0.007	-0.001	-0.003
Eurozone × CBPP2 Ann. [p,q]	0.014	0.024	0.003	0.023
Eurozone × CBPP2 Details Ann. [p,q]	-0.001	-0.076***	0.001	0.000
Eurozone × Draghi Statement [p,q]	0.013	0.001	0.007	0.012
Eurozone × OMT Indication [p,q]	0.035**	0.000	-0.024*	0.029*
Eurozone × OMT Ann. [p,q]	0.001	0.005	0.006	0.001
Eurozone × CBPP3 Ann. [p,q]	-0.006	0.004	0.019	-0.011
Eurozone × CBPP3 Details Ann. [p,q]	-0.004	0.005	0.004	0.003
Eurozone × PSPP Ann. [p,q]	-0.003	0.007	-0.002	0.001
Germany				
Eurozone × CBPP1 Ann. [p,q]	-0.057**	-0.052**	-0.022	-0.047**
Eurozone × CBPP1 Details Ann. [p,q]	-0.083***	-0.048**	-0.039	-0.054**
Eurozone × SMP Ann. [p,q]	-0.015	-0.013	0.024	-0.014
Eurozone × SMP Reactivation [p,q]	-0.000	-0.003	-0.002	0.011
Eurozone × CBPP2 Ann. [p,q]	-0.020	-0.010	0.009	-0.006
Eurozone × CBPP2 Details Ann. [p,q]	-0.009	0.005	-0.020	-0.000
Eurozone × Draghi Statement [p,q]	-0.000	0.000	-0.012	0.009
Eurozone × OMT Indication [p,q]	-0.008	0.005	0.009	-0.001
Eurozone × OMT Ann. [p,q]	0.011	0.019	-0.001	0.024
Eurozone × CBPP3 Ann. [p,q]	0.019	0.016	0.000	0.017
Eurozone × CBPP3 Details Ann. [p,q]	0.014	0.014	0.008	0.016
Eurozone × PSPP Ann. [p,q]	0.011	0.018	0.003	0.013
Netherlands				
Eurozone × CBPP1 Ann. [p,q]	0.013	-0.020	0.012	-0.034
Eurozone × CBPP1 Details Ann. [p,q]	-0.038	-0.020	-0.019	-0.010
Eurozone × SMP Ann. [p,q]	-0.000	-0.004	0.007	0.003
Eurozone × SMP Reactivation [p,q]	-0.011	-0.003	-0.002	-0.004
Eurozone × CBPP2 Ann. [p,q]	0.002	-0.009	-0.014	0.000

Eurozone × CBPP2 Details Ann. [p,q]	-0.003	0.000	0.007	-0.015
Eurozone × Draghi Statement [p,q]	0.019	0.008	0.004	-0.001
Eurozone × OMT Indication [p,q]	0.027	-0.002	-0.024	0.017
Eurozone × OMT Ann. [p,q]	0.001	0.001	0.007	-0.004
Eurozone × CBPP3 Ann. [p,q]	-0.004	-0.001	0.013	-0.008
Eurozone × CBPP3 Details Ann. [p,q]	-0.005	-0.002	0.005	-0.002
Eurozone × PSPP Ann. [p,q]	-0.012	0.024	0.006	-0.010

The regression results show the impact on individual covered bonds' yield spread versus the asset swap with an equivalent maturity, which serves as the independent variable. Regressions (30) through (33) vary in the event windows [p,q] considered for the analysis of announcement effects. The sample period is from June 12, 2008, to June 30, 2015. The controls variables Time to Maturity, Bid-Ask-Spread, Sovereign vs. Germany, Banking Sector Risk, and FX SWAP equiv.; the overall day effects for CBPP1 to CBPP3 and their technical detail announcements; the SMP and its reactivation; and the OMT announcements are omitted for ease of reading. The same holds true for Rating Dummies, Country & Sector Dummies, and the Individual Quarter Dummies. The regressions comprise 237 covered bonds (R^2 = 45.2%) for Austria, 415 (R^2 = 48.2 to 48.4%) for France, 494 (R^2 = 50.7%) for Germany, and 230 (R^2 = 46.4%) for the Netherlands. Significance levels: * 0.10, ** 0.05, *** 0.01.

Table 21: Individual Country Regression Results for Periphery Countries

	(34) [-5,-1]	(35) [-2,2]	(36) [0,0]	(37) [1,5]
Spain				
Eurozone × CBPP1 Ann. [p,q]	-0.006	-0.030*	0.043**	-0.037**
Eurozone × CBPP1 Details Ann. [p,q]	-0.001	0.004	-0.011	0.024
Eurozone × SMP Ann. [p,q]	0.074***	0.041**	-0.056***	-0.022
Eurozone × SMP Reactivation [p,q]	0.010	0.001	-0.013	0.003
Eurozone × CBPP2 Ann. [p,q]	-0.003	0.002	0.007	-0.003
Eurozone × CBPP2 Details Ann. [p,q]	-0.008	-0.056***	-0.005	0.008
Eurozone × Draghi Statement [p,q]	0.045***	0.062***	0.013	0.055***
Eurozone × OMT Indication [p,q]	0.047***	0.045***	0.030**	0.028*
Eurozone × OMT Ann. [p,q]	0.015	0.014	0.035***	0.001
Eurozone × CBPP3 Ann. [p,q]	0.014	0.008	0.007	-0.024
Eurozone × CBPP3 Details Ann. [p,q]	0.011	0.006	0.004	-0.014
Eurozone × PSPP Ann. [p,q]	0.000	-0.007	0.006	-0.004
Ireland				
Eurozone × CBPP1 Ann. [p,q]	-0.061	-0.027	0.117***	-0.021
Eurozone × CBPP1 Details Ann. [p,q]	0.051	-0.011	-0.018	0.044
Eurozone × SMP Ann. [p,q]	0.022	0.011	-0.018	-0.003
Eurozone × SMP Reactivation [p,q]	-0.041	0.029	-0.064	0.141***
Eurozone × CBPP2 Ann. [p,q]	0.054	0.059	-0.014	0.030
Eurozone × CBPP2 Details Ann. [p,q]	-0.021	0.054	0.012	-0.008
Eurozone × Draghi Statement [p,q]	-0.004	0.044	-0.005	0.046
Eurozone × OMT Indication [p,q]	0.007	0.068	0.008	0.048
Eurozone × OMT Ann. [p,q]	0.018	0.010	0.004	0.010
Eurozone × CBPP3 Ann. [p,q]	0.006	-0.007	0.007	-0.020
Eurozone × CBPP3 Details Ann. [p,q]	0.006	0.001	-0.004	-0.004
Eurozone × PSPP Ann. [p,q]	-0.007	-0.007	0.005	-0.011
Italy				
Eurozone × CBPP1 Ann. [p,q]	-0.010	-0.021	-0.013	-0.000
Eurozone × CBPP1 Details Ann. [p,q]	0.001	0.006	0.003	-0.013
Eurozone × SMP Ann. [p,q]	-0.020	0.038	0.026	-0.006
Eurozone × SMP Reactivation [p,q]	-0.042	-0.006	0.022	0.011
Eurozone × CBPP2 Ann. [p,q]	0.014	0.017	0.003	0.014
Eurozone × CBPP2 Details Ann. [p,q]	-0.012	-0.391***	0.044	-0.067**
Eurozone × Draghi Statement [p,q]	0.019	0.005	0.043*	0.059**
Eurozone × OMT Indication [p,q]	0.099***	0.012	-0.027	0.078***
Eurozone × OMT Ann. [p,q]	0.019	0.035	0.018	0.009
Eurozone × CBPP3 Ann. [p,q]	0.002	0.000	0.013	-0.029
Eurozone × CBPP3 Details Ann. [p,q]	0.006	0.007	-0.000	-0.014
Eurozone × PSPP Ann. [p,q]	-0.001	-0.014	-0.001	0.000
Portugal				
Eurozone × CBPP1 Ann. [p,q]	-0.032	0.009	0.019	-0.022
Eurozone × CBPP1 Details Ann. [p,q]	-0.001	0.020	-0.021	0.012
Eurozone × SMP Ann. [p,q]	0.314***	0.041	-0.260***	-0.043
Eurozone × SMP Reactivation [p,q]	-0.155***	0.026	-0.091**	0.161***
Eurozone × CBPP2 Ann. [p,q]	0.089**	-0.007	-0.093**	0.079*

Eurozone × CBPP2 Details Ann. [p,q]	0.044	0.001	0.021	-0.031
Eurozone × Draghi Statement [p,q]	0.012	-0.039	-0.059	0.054
Eurozone × OMT Indication [p,q]	-0.050	-0.102*	0.060	-0.017
Eurozone × OMT Ann. [p,q]	0.180***	0.030	-0.151***	0.079*
Eurozone × CBPP3 Ann. [p,q]	0.015	0.001	-0.013	-0.017
Eurozone × CBPP3 Details Ann. [p,q]	0.005	-0.008	0.010	-0.012
Eurozone × EAPP Ann. [p,q]	-0.002	0.004	-0.005	-0.021

The regression results show the impact on individual covered bonds' yield spread versus the asset swap with an equivalent maturity, which serves as the independent variable. Regressions (34) through (37) vary in the event windows [p,q] considered for the analysis of announcement effects. The sample period is from June 12, 2008, to June 30, 2015. The controls variables Time to Maturity, Bid-Ask-Spread, Sovereign vs. Germany, Banking Sector Risk, and FX SWAP equiv.; the overall day effects for CBPP1 to CBPP3 and their technical detail announcements; the SMP and its reactivation; and the OMT announcements are omitted for ease of reading. The same holds true for Rating Dummies, Country & Sector Dummies, and the Individual Quarter Dummies. The regressions comprise 237 covered bonds (R^2 = 45.2%) for Spain, 46 (R^2 = 46.3 to 46.4%) for Ireland, 254 (R^2 = 46.4 to 46.7%) for Italy, and 41 (R^2 = 55.2 to 55.5%) for Portugal. Significance levels: * 0.10, ** 0.05, *** 0.01.

As expected, we do not observe any effect on the announcement of CBPP2. However, for CBPP3, we find a 2-bp tightening of periphery country spreads, while core country spreads remain unchanged. This result can be explained by increased investor appetite for riskier periphery covered bonds, which are expected to outperform under ECB purchases.

In line with our expectations, we do not note any significant effects for the announcements of the technical details of either CBPP1 or CBPP3; the degree of new information contained was marginal. However, the German covered bond spreads are an exception, in that they tightened by 5 bps upon the announcement of the technical details of CBPP1.

The technical details of CBPP2 led to isolated incidents of spread tightening in the [-2,2]-day event window of 7 bps and 3 bps for the core and periphery countries, respectively. This result indicates that the easing of eligibility criteria came to the market as a positive surprise. In fact, Table 22 indicates a 9-bp tightening for covered bonds with a remaining maturity of less than three years, whose eligibility under CBPP2 was a surprise to the market.

Table 22: Maturity Effects for All Countries

	(38) **[-5,-1]**	(39) **[-2,2]**	(40) **[0,0]**	(41) **[1,5]**
1-3 years				
Eurozone × CBPP1 Ann. [p,q]	-0.018	-0.005	0.013	-0.018
Eurozone × CBPP1 Details Ann. [p,q]	-0.014	0.009	-0.001	-0.021
Eurozone × SMP Ann. [p,q]	0.012	0.017	0.006	-0.000
Eurozone × SMP Reactivation [p,q]	-0.037	0.001	0.025	0.010
Eurozone × CBPP2 Ann. [p,q]	0.013	0.009	-0.007	0.024
Eurozone × CBPP2 Details Ann. [p,q]	0.008	-0.085**	-0.005	-0.005
Eurozone × Draghi Statement [p,q]	0.039	0.075**	0.016	0.106***
Eurozone × OMT Indication [p,q]	0.093**	0.081**	-0.013	0.126***
Eurozone × OMT Ann. [p,q]	0.044	0.052	0.017	0.044
Eurozone × CBPP3 Ann. [p,q]	-0.002	0.002	0.011	-0.016
Eurozone × CBPP3 Details Ann. [p,q]	-0.001	0.001	-0.003	-0.002
Eurozone × PSPP Ann. [p,q]	-0.006	-0.015	-0.000	-0.005

The regression results show the impact on individual covered bonds' yield spread versus the asset swap with an equivalent maturity, which serves as the independent variable. Regressions (38) through (41) vary in the event windows [p,q] considered for the analysis of announcement effects. The sample period is from June 12, 2008, to June 30, 2015. The controls variables Time to Maturity, Bid-Ask-Spread, Sovereign vs. Germany, Banking Sector Risk, and FX SWAP equiv.; the overall day effects for CBPP1 to CBPP3 and their technical detail announcements; the SMP and its reactivation; and the OMT announcements are omitted for ease of reading. The same holds true for Rating Dummies, Country & Sector Dummies, and the Individual Quarter Dummies. The regression comprises 762 covered bonds (R^2 = 71.7 to 71.8%) for maturities of one year to three years. Significance levels: * 0.10, ** 0.05, *** 0.01.

For the all other announcement effects, we are not able to draw a conclusion about a stronger or weaker reaction to ECB unconventional monetary policy depending on remaining time to maturity. We cannot, therefore, confirm the results of Gibson et al. (2016), who find a larger price effect for the purchase of covered bonds with longer maturity.[88]

With respect to differences in covered bond ratings, we note a 3-bp tightening for AAA-rated covered bonds upon the announcement of CBPP1 that is not matched by sub-AAA covered bonds; however, we are not able to derive any pattern for systematic differences between AAA and lower-rated covered bonds.[89]

[88] They consider maturities longer than 10.5 years, which are not included in our sample; yet, we assume the logic holds.

[89] The results are available upon request.

For announcements of sovereign bond purchase programs, we observe an overall tightening of covered bond spreads of 3 bps upon the announcement of the SMP for the [0,0]-day event window. This result remains slightly below the widening of the [-5,-1]-day event window. While this holds true with a magnitude of 9 bps for the periphery countries, we do not observe such an effect for the core countries. Our results are therefore very different from those of Szczerbowicz (2015), who identifies a covered bond tightening of 19 bps for the [0,0]-day event window upon the announcement of the SMP for euro-denominated covered bonds. We attribute this effect to the clear focus of the SMP on periphery markets. The spillover mechanism from sovereign bond markets also seems to be very efficient, compared to covered bond market announcements, which appear to reflect the positive news only in a wider event window. This is particularly the case for Spanish and Portuguese covered bonds, in which the announcement led to a spread tightening, almost offsetting the widening of the previous week, as shown in the [-5,1]-day event window.

The three events in connection with the OMT have no significant effect on the overall and core covered bond markets. However, the spreads gradually widen upon and around Draghi's speech and the indication of the OMT by 4 bps and 3 bps, respectively, for the periphery countries. We attribute these results to the different risk preferences of investors, who react by shifting assets from dual recourse covered bonds to sovereign bonds, which are expected to outperform upon ECB safeguarding. We particularly attribute the positive spread changes of Spanish and Italian covered bonds around all three events in relation with the OMT to this change in investor risk preference. While Irish covered bonds did not show any reaction to these announcements, the actual OMT announcement tightened spreads in the [0,0]-day event window by 15 bps, thereby relaxing almost all the tension that had built up in the week before the announcement by 18 bps.

Finally, we do not find any significant effects due to the announcement of the PSPP. Our results are therefore in line with those of Kilponen et al. (2015), in that the market effect of unconventional policy measures is the strongest for those markets toward which the instruments are geared.

Robustness Tests

Our finding that covered bond spreads did not widen upon the announcement of all unconventional monetary policy announcements targeted at covered bond markets is contrary to our expectations. Beyond our conclusion that the average market reaction upon the unconventional monetary policy announcements has not been significant, we identify two alternative reasons.

First, announcement effects could already have been absorbed by different variables, such as *Sovereign vs. Germany*. However, we argue that sovereign risk is a substantial pricing component of covered bonds and should not be omitted during times of sovereign debt crises.

Second, the chosen control group might not be as unbiased as expected. In that case, we would expect covered bond yields issued by non-eurozone banks to react to unconventional monetary policy announcements via portfolio rebalancing and therefore be affected in the same direction as eurozone covered bonds. These spillovers would be a sign of an efficient international covered bond market. However, we are not able to draw on any previous literature on this topic with regard to the covered bond market.

We ran further robustness tests. We considered a number of additional variables, including bond coupon rates to account for differences in tax treatment (Prokopczuk & Vonhoff, 2012), as well as the accrued interest as an additional pricing measure. We further included the 3M interbank lending rate and the 3M overnight index swap, as well as the difference between these two, as a proxy for interbank credit risk (Prokopczuk & Vonhoff, 2012; Longstaff & Schwartz, 1995; Campbell & Taksler, 2003) in our model. None of these measures were able to improve model quality beyond the variables chosen.

In addition to *Bid-Ask-Spread* as our liquidity measure, we tested Roll's (1984) liquidity measure (Dick-Nielsen et al., 2009; Buchholst et al., 2010), as well as the nominal volume of each covered bond and several combinations thereof. The nominal volume would have served as a measure of idiosyncratic risk, as employed by Prokopczuk and Vonhoff (2012) and tested for by Delatte et al. (2016). However, all of these models have been proven inferior to the one presented. The same holds true for the slope of the swap curve and the natural logarithm of the local equity index, which account for the condition of the local economy and capital markets.

6.4 Subsidiary Conclusion

We analyze the announcement effects of the ECB's unconventional monetary policy measures (CBPP1 to CBPP3, the SMP, OMT, and the PSPP) between June 2008 and June 2015. We employ a difference-in-difference estimator using a control group of non-eurozone covered bonds denominated in euros to establish a causal relationship between the announcements and the yield spreads for covered bonds eligible for Eurosystem purchases.

We find that the first CBPP achieved its goal of tightening the covered bond spreads by approximately 3 bps in the [-2,2]-day event window for the eurozone. This amount is smaller than the 12 bps reported by Beirne et al. (2011) but similar to the finding of Szczerbowicz (2015) for CBPP1 and CBPP2. We attribute the differences with Beirne et al. to the differing methodology and introduction of the asset swap as a difference estimator. In line with our expectation of a marginal information transmission upon the announcement of CBPP2, we do not find a significant impact on covered bond spreads. The same holds true for CBPP3.

Announcements of the technical details of CBPPs did not lead to market reactions. An exception is the unexpected inclusion of covered bonds with short maturities of one year to three years within the scope of eligibility for CBPP2, leading to a 9-bp tightening in the [-2,2]-day event window for that particular group of bonds.

We find significant tightening of covered bond spreads upon the announcement of the SMP on the event day. However, it merely offsets the spread widening prior to the announcement, which can be attributed to periphery countries. We generally find no tightening effects for the OMT program but instead report widening spreads for the periphery countries, which we attribute to changes in investor portfolio rebalancing. On the contrary, the covered bond markets of the core countries were not affected by sovereign bond purchase announcements.

7 Monetary Policy Implications

In drawing conclusions for the analyses presented, it is essential to not only consider the goals of the three CBPPs as put forward by the ECB, but instead to consider capital market and banking sector conditions and presenting the drivers of the ECB's decision to conduct the programs.

7.1 Periods of Bank Funding Stress

The announcement of CBPP1 in May 2009 has led to a tightening of eurozone covered bond spreads. Beirne et al. (2011) quantify it to 12 bps, while Szczerbowicz (2015) finds a 4-bp tightening versus Bunds on the event day. This study determines a tightening of 10 bps versus British covered bonds and a 3-bp tightening of covered bond spreads against the asset swap compared to a wider group of non-eurozone countries in a [2,2]-day event window. We therefore identify an easing of bank funding conditions due to the announcement of covered bond purchases, when bank funding was severely stressed. This result is confirmed by Kettemann and Krogstrup (2011) who find a 10-bp tightening of covered bond spreads for the day of the Swiss National Bank's program announcement.

In line with efficient market hypothesis, announcements are most effective when they arrive unexpectedly. As CBPP1 has been the ECB's first outright purchase program and therefore also its first one acquiring covered bonds, the surprise occurred not only in timing, but also in its specification. This evidence confirms Bluwstein and Canova's (2016) observation that surprise announcements can potentially trigger a market reaction comparable to that of conventional monetary policy.

We are not able to extend this effect to a continued re-balancing when the purchases are taking place. Covered bond markets seem to have priced in the whole effect upon the information reaching the public domain. However, we are able to demonstrate that this initial announcement lasts for approximately seven weeks, before its effects diminish due to new information.

H. Markmann, *Covered Bonds under Unconventional Monetary Policy*,
Essays in Real Estate Research 14,
https://doi.org/10.1007/978-3-658-20975-9_7

For CBPP1, we do not notice secondary market rebalancing effects among maturities, ratings, or countries. We did not test for liquidity measures and can therefore not conclude on the liquidity channel of unconventional monetary policy. Considering the program's impact on the interest term structure, Szczerbowicz (2015) finds a 5-bp reduction of eurozone sovereign bond spreads upon the announcement of CBPP1 and CBPP2 with the largest impacts for Greece, Italy, and Spain. Falagiarda and Reitz (2015), however, find CBPP1 and CBPP2 not to have had an impact on sovereign yields of stressed countries. This is confirmed by Watfe (2015) for a broader set of sovereign countries.

We find a slight increase of covered bond yields versus covered bonds from the United Kingdom for the implementation of the first two CBPPs. This is contrary to our expectation, and Krishnamurthy and Vissing-Jorgensen's (2011) finding of a continued decrease in interest rates for QE1.

Regarding CBPP1's primary market impact, Szczerbowicz (2015) finds a 7 bps reduction of the counterparty risk measure (Libor-OIS) upon the announcements of CBPP1 and CBPP2. This re-instated confidence eases bank's funding conditions substantially by means of decreased credit risk. Controlling for the improvement in bank funding conditions,[90] we find CBPP1 to have been successful in restoring the primary covered bond market's functionality. In fact, we find each euro-billion in primary bond purchases to have triggered an additional €6.8 billion in covered bond emissions, which translates to approximately 69% of all eligible emissions during the period of CBPP1. This effect is even stronger for periphery countries with a marginal emission effect of 14.3x.

The achievement of CBPP1 was the calming of banking sector stress, leading to improved investor confidence in the covered bond market, additional covered bond emissions, and thereby eased bank funding conditions. This led to a dampening of the banking portion of the GFC and let to avoid new crisis peaks on the grounds of lacking funding. The €60 billion employed therefore seem to have been a rather low investment by the Eurosystem. Assuming a spread tightening to be the main goal of the ECB, a 3 to 10-bp tightening seems to remain shy of a substantial improvement of funding conditions and thereby bank lending. Unfortunately, there is no study available considering the programs impact

[90] The correlation coefficient between the Libor-OIS spread and the Banking Sector Risk is 0.72 for the time period from January 2006 to June 2015.

on real economy lending. We therefore conclude CBPP1 to have been very effective in promoting covered bond emissions, when capital markets are stalling due to a stressed banking sector, and to lead to a 3 to 10-bp tightening upon an unexpected program announcement.

7.2 Sovereign Debt Crises

The second CBPP was largely expected by capital markets, and we cannot find any impact of its announcement on market spreads against the swap rate and a small tightening of 4 bps tightening against covered bonds from the United Kingdom. However, the inclusion of covered bonds with a one to three year maturity under CBPP2 eligibility criteria reached markets at surprise and we observe a 9 bps tightening for that market segment. We neither find an impact on primary market activity.

The probability of success of CBPP2 has largely been expected to be small, due to the fact that the program was anticipated, and covered bond markets did not exhibit adverse conditions, which would prohibit emissions. However, emission activity in the unsecured bond segment appeared impaired but the program was not geared towards that market. While market participants recall a number of new emissions being floated upon the announcement of CBPP2, these are considered to having been upheld to await a better environment, rather than being enabled by the program. The timely proximity of the LTRO2 may have also re-directed banks to obtain liquidity through that channel rather than issuing covered bonds (Hauser & Burkert, 2012).

Considering the announcement of CBPP2 as part of the ECB's broader unconventional monetary policy measures, the findings of Szczerbowicz (2015), Falagiarda & Reitz (2015), and Watfe (2015) hold. In the contrary direction, Szczerbowicz (2015) finds a 19-bp tightening of the covered bond spreads upon the announcement of the SMP and a 6-bp tightening upon the announcement of the OMT for eurozone covered bonds. While we find a 9-bp tightening of covered bonds spreads from periphery countries upon the announcement of SMP. This, however, merely offsets the widening of the previous week.

We find an indication for portfolio (re-)balancing in that covered bond spreads of periphery countries increase upon Draghi's "whatever it takes"-speech and the ECB's indication of the OMT. We attribute the observed spread increases to a rebalancing into periphery sovereign debt, which was expected to become less risky upon the announcements. Additionally, the yield for German covered bonds increases by 10 bps in the medium term, suggesting a (re-)balancing towards more risky markets.

In summary the unconventional monetary policy measures taken during the sovereign debt crisis, had a limited impact on the covered bond market, as it was in rather sound condition. Particularly, the measures undertaken did not improve the underlying market deficiencies, namely the sovereign debt crisis and banks inability to attain unsecured funding.

7.3 Periods of Deflationary Pressure

The announcements of the TLTRO and CBPP3 marked the beginning of the ECB's implementation of an explicit strategy to expand the monetary base and therefore to sustainably lower the long-term interest rate. By this time, the covered bond market was in good health, since spreads were close to the pre-GFC levels and the emission market was active. The outright purchase of covered bonds has been initiated, on the basis of the ECB having had experience in that market, the market is large enough to absorb central bank sized funds, and quickly affects banks and thereby their ability to lower lending rates.

Considering the covered bond market specifically, we find no announcement effects and no impact of actual purchases. Additionally, the primary market did not show reactions to primary market purchases of the Eurosystem. While unconventional monetary policy would lead to the expectation of a stronger effect for long-term bonds, we cannot confirm this expectation.

Due to the timely proximity, the literature on CBPP3's effect on sovereign bonds is limited to Watfe (2015), who does not finds a change in sovereign bond spreads triggered by the announcement of CBPP3.

While the ECB is currently undertaking a prime example for unconventional monetary policy, it may be prone to be facing a couple difficulties previously articulated, particularly with respect to the covered bond sector: Hannoun (2012) mentions delays in balance sheet adjustments in the economy, enhanced risk taking and more leverage, which during the course of asset price inflation might lead to bubble developments (Sachs, 2012). The author continues to point out that markets lose their capacity for price discovery and central banks may play a too dominant role in certain markets.

While the former two arguments clearly relate to the real estate and capital markets, of which particularly the latter relates to the covered bond market. While a potential real estate bubble might lead to a renewed housing and banking crisis, and a dysfunctional covered bond market. As Figure 16 shows, the share of the Eurosystem's holdings of the total euro-denominated market increased to 29% in October 2015 (Beaumont, 2015) and would rise to 54% under a continued rate of purchases by the end of 2016.[91] Strong fear of a too dominant a market position of the Eurosystem has been echoed by the market participants' opinion aggregated in Melm, Rudolf, and Schuller (2016), however, in order to achieve its aims under its unconventional monetary policy the ECB seems to perceive potential negative effects as collateral damage.

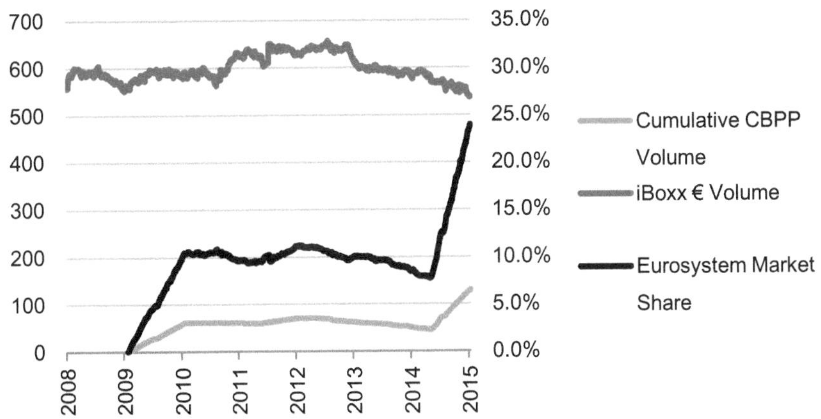

Figure 16: Eurosystem Market Share of Covered Bond Market
Cumulative CBPP volumes as per held in the Eurosystem balance sheet and the market defined as the market value of all Markit iBoxx euro covered bond constituents from the eurozone. Source: Own illustration based on Beaumont (2015)

91 Assuming a constant volume of Euro-denominated benchmark covered bonds outstanding and part of the Markit iBoxx index, monthly purchases under CBPP3 of €9 billion, and no maturing covered bonds already held by the Eurosystem.

8 Conclusion

Our analysis on the primary and secondary covered bond markets leads us to realize a number of research deficiencies and opportunities for future research. A summary of the analysis follows.

8.1 Research Deficiencies and Opportunities

We have identified five potential influences of three CBPPs on covered bond yields (Section 3.4.2). However, in our analysis, we are limited to two. First, we have not identified the effect the Eurosystem acting as an anchor investor on the pricing of covered bond emission and its effect to the composition of the investor group. Second, we do not determine the price impact of the additional covered bond supply exerted, and third, we do not consider liquidity considerations.

The omission of liquidity considerations is also present in the broader literature on covered bonds and presents a sizable research opportunity. Similarly, a number of issues pertaining to covered bond market structure are not yet analyzed and weaken the basis upon which we are drawing our conclusions. These include pricing models on a trade-by-trade basis, and the efficiency of the covered bond market. Part of the latter are spillover effects between covered and sovereign debt markets, as well as covered bond markets of different countries and different credit risk.

The event study analyses employed rely on a sound expectation of the reaction behavior of the covered bond market in terms of speed of reaction, market resilience, and potential overshooting effect. No such body of literature exists yet.

With respect to the primary market, we consider covered bonds in an isolated fashion, while Beirne et al. (2011) find a crowding out effect of unsecured bonds in favor of covered bonds. A full bank funding model would be able to shed further light on this question including pricing and availability criteria. The same holds true for the inclusion of the availability of repo facilities, such as LTRO and the easing of collateral restrictions.

H. Markmann, *Covered Bonds under Unconventional Monetary Policy*,
Essays in Real Estate Research 14,
https://doi.org/10.1007/978-3-658-20975-9_8

Our analysis is currently limited on immediate effects of CBPPs in the covered bond market, which is emission volumes and spreads. However, the goals set forward by the ECB claim second and third level goals of a low interest term structure and enhanced lending to the real economy. We are not able to draw conclusions about these effects, but only assume its effects if the traditional transmission mechanism holds.

The results of our analyses suggest outright covered bond purchases to be successful when they are targeted at reviving a dysfunctional covered bond market, or arrive to the market at surprise.[92] However, this leads to a dilemma: First, if the outright covered bond purchases are successful at reviving a dysfunctional market, why did the unexpected inclusion of short-term covered bonds under CBPP lead to a reduction in spreads? Second, if outright covered bond purchases are successful when they arrive to the market at surprise, has the surprise element for CBPP3 already diminished? If so, would similar programs, now part of the central bank's toolbox, ever be unexpected again?

8.2 Summary

We study the behavior of covered bonds through the GFC to 2015Q2 and put an emphasis on their reaction to the ECB's unconventional monetary policy measures. The Eurosystem's CBPPs were implemented during three different stages of the GFC and under different macro-economic conditions. We therefore scrutinize the programs' effectiveness, considering these conditions and including the findings of the literature.

Building on the ECB's goals in conducting CBPPs, and the prevalent literature on covered bonds and unconventional monetary policy, we analyze primary and secondary market effects. We are particularly interested in covered bond emission volume and spread changes upon the announcement and implementation of unconventional monetary policy interventions. We honor that our research does not allow for a conclusive statement on the effectiveness of CBPPs, but provides a basis for further research. Selected areas for future research contain covered bond liquidity, spillover effects within covered bond and with sov-

[92] CBPP1 arrived to the market at surprise and the market was dysfunctional, while the inclusion of covered bonds with a maturity of 1-3 years in the technical details of CBPP2 arrived at surprise.

ereign bond markets, as well as banks choices among capital market funding instruments.

Our results indicate CBPP1 to have been successful in restoring the primary covered bond market functionality, and we quantify additional covered bond emissions to €103 billion, equivalent to 6.3-fold the amount directed to primary covered bond purchases. This effect is even stronger for periphery countries with an emission multiplier of the 14.3-fold. Some of this effect may be due to the decreased secondary market spread, which we found to drop by 3 bps upon the announcement. We find the 10 bps lower spread versus covered bonds from the United Kingdom to sustain for seven weeks. The program has therefore been successful in overcoming severe difficulties in banks attaining capital market funding.

CBPP2 did not trigger any additional funding activity in the covered bond market. Additionally, secondary market spreads did not or only slightly react to the announcement of the program, which was largely expected by market participants, and not equipped to solve the prevalent sovereign debt crisis, nor the dysfunctional market for unsecured bank debt. The role of repo-transactions remains unclear in this context.

CBPP3 was implemented to increase the monetary base, and to lower the interest term structure, which is in line with unconventional monetary policy theory. We find no impact on either primary or secondary markets. Instead, we find indications for portfolio (re-)balancing between different covered bond market segments and the sovereign bond market.

While heterogeneous, literature suggests the announcements of CBPPs not to have led to a decrease in the sovereign bond term structure, and therefore not to have been successful under unconventional monetary policy's main transmission mechanism. The reaction of covered bond markets to outright sovereign bond purchases is mixed and we find a 6-bp tightening for periphery countries due to the announcement of the SMP, which is line with Falagiarda and Reitz (2015).

Outright bond purchases are therefore appropriate to restore dysfunctional capital markets, particularly the covered bond market. However, their suitability in lowering the interest term structure in covered and more so in sovereign bond markets is limited.

List of References

Acharya, V.V., & Pedersen, L.H. (2005). Asset pricing with liquidity risk. *Journal of Financial Economics*, 77 (2), 375-410.

Altavilla, C., Giannone, D., & Lenza, M. (2016). The financial and macroeconomic effects of OMT announcements. *International Journal of Central Banking, 12(3),* 29-57.

Alter, A., & Beyer, A. (2014). The dynamics of spillover effects during the European sovereign debt turmoil. *Journal of Banking and Finance*, 42, 134-153.

Anand, K., Chapman, J., & Gai, P. (2012). Covered bonds, core markets, and financial stability. *SFB 649 Discussion Paper, 2012-065.*

Arghyrou, M. G., & Kontonikas, A. (2012). The EMU sovereign-debt crisis: Fundamentals, expectations and contagion. *Journal of International Financial Markets, Institutions and Money, 22(4)*, 658-677.

Backus, D., & Wright, J. (2007). Cracking the Conundrum. *Brookings Papers on Economic Activity, 2007-1*, 293-329.

Bank of International Settlements (2013). *Basel III: The Liquidity Coverage Ratio and liquidity risk monitoring*. January 2013. Retrieved on January 13, 2017 from http://www.bis.org/publ/bcbs238.pdf.

Bauer, M.D., & Rudebusch, G.D. (2011). The Signaling channel for Federal Reserve Bond Purchases. *Federal Reserve Bank of San Francisco Working Paper*, 2011-32.

Beaumont, J. (2015). CBPP3 – winding down in 2016?. ABN Amro – Covered Bond Watch, on November 11, 2016 from: retrieved http://nordic-fi.com/ecb-unveils-cbpp3-alongside-abs-buying-but-few-details/.

Beirne, J., Dalitz, L., Ejsing, J., Grothe, M., Manganelli, S., Monar, F., ... Vong, T. (2011). The impact of the Eurosystem's covered bond purchase programme on the primary and secondary markets. *Occasional Paper Series 122.*

Bernanke, B.S. (2002). Deflation: Making Sure 'It' Doesn't Happen Here. Speech at the *National Economists Club*, Washington, DC, November 21,

H. Markmann, *Covered Bonds under Unconventional Monetary Policy*,
Essays in Real Estate Research 14,
https://doi.org/10.1007/978-3-658-20975-9

2002; retrieved on February 14, 2017 www.federalreserve.gov/boarddocs /speeches/2002/20021121/default.htm.

Bernoth, K., & Erdogan, B. (2012). Sovereign bond yield spreads: A time-varying coefficient approach. *Journal of International Money and Finance*, 31, 639-656.

Birkmeyer, J., & Herbert, T. (2002). Jumbo Pfandbrief spreads: Everything new, everything different or everything as it was? *The Pfandbrief*, 7, 69–77.

Bluwstein, K., & Canova, F. (2016). Beggar Thy-Neighbor? The International Effects of ECB Unconventional Monetary Policy Measures. *International Journal of Central Banking*, 12(3), 69-120.

Breger, L., & Stovel, D. (2004). Agency Ratings in the Pfandbrief Market. *Journal of Portfolio Management*, 30, 239-243.

Brunnermeier, M.K., & Pedersen, L.H. (2009). Market Liquidity and Funding Liquidity. *Review of Financial Studies*, 22(6), 2201-2238.

Buchholst, B.V., Gyntelberg, J., & Sangill, T. (2010). Liquidity of Danish government and covered bonds - before, during and after the financial crisis – preliminary findings. *Working Paper 70*, Danmarks Nationalbank.

Burmeister, R. (2009). Introduction. In European Covered Bond Council, *2009 ECBC European Covered Bond Fact Book* (pp. 25-26).

Burmeister, R., Grossmann, R., & Stöcker, O. (2011). Overview of Covered Bonds. In European Covered Bond Council, 2011 *ECBC European Covered Bond Fact Book* (pp. 97-108).

Campbell, J.Y., & Taksler, G.B. (2003). Equity volatility and corporate bond yields. *Journal of Finance*, 58(6), 2321–2349.

Carbo-Valverde, S., Rosen, R., & Rogríguez-Fernández, F. (2011). Are covered bonds a substitute for mortgage-backed securities? *Federal Reserve Bank of Chicago Working Paper*, 2011-14.

Caruana, J., & van Rixtel, A. (2011). International financial markets and bank funding in the euro area: dynamics and participants. *Bank for International Settlements*.

Chordia, T., Sarkar, A., & Subrahmanyam, A. (2005). An Empirical Analysis of Stock and Bond Market Liquidity. *Review of Financial Studies*, 18(1), 85-129.

Christensen, J.H.E., & Gillan, J.M. (2016). Does Quantitative Easing Affect Market Liquidity?. *Federal Reserve of San Francisco – Working Paper Series*, Working Paper 2013-26.

Commandeur, J.J.F., & Koopman, S.J. (2007). *An Introduction to State Space Time Series Analysis*. Oxford and New York: Oxford University Press.

Constâncio, V. (2015). Assessing the new phase of unconventional monetary policy at the ECB. Panel remarks at the *Annual Congress of the European Economic Association*, University of Mannheim, August 25, 2015. Retrieved on February 13, 2017 from: https://www.ecb.europa.eu/press/key/date/2015/html/sp150825.en.html.

Costa, C. (2016). Who Buys Covered Bonds?. In European Covered Bond Council, *2016 ECBC European Covered Bond Fact Book* (pp. 142-144).

Cour-Thimann, P., & Winkler, B. (2013). The ECB's Non-Standard Monetary Policy Measures – The Role of Intuitional Factors and Financial Structure. *European Central Bank Working Paper Series*, 1528(April 2013).

Credit Suisse (2011). *Covered Bonds – Insight*. Retrieved from: https://doc.research-and-analytics.csfb.com/docView?language=ENG &format=PDF&document_id=804522140&source_id=em&serialid=Wt8xlI 6QhoCGTjUIwbidjIP%2BqRjTuIMysxdhlk7Jd78%3D.

Creel, J., Hubert, P., & Viennot, M. (2013). Assessing the Interest Rate and Bank Lending Channels of ECB Monetary Policies. Working Paper.

De Pooter, M., DeSimone, R., Martin, R.F., & Pruitt, S. (2015). Cheap Talk and the Efficacy of the ECB's Securities Market Programme: Did Bond Purchases Matter? *International Finance Discussion Papers 1139*.

Delatte, A.-L., Fouquau, J., & Portes, R. (2016). Regime-Dependent Sovereign Risk Pricing during the Euro Crisis. *Review of Finance*, First published online October 10, 2016.

Deutsche Bundesbank (2016). *2015 Annual Report*, Frankfurt: Deutsche Bundesbank.

Dick-Nielsen, J., Gyntelberg, J., & Sangill, T. (2012). Liquidity in government versus covered bond markets. *Dansmarks Nationalbank Working Papers*, 83.

Dierks, L., & Somerville, J. (2012). Covered bonds in sovereign debt crisis. In European Covered Bond Council, *2012 ECBC European Covered Bond Fact Book* (pp. 39-46).

Diez, F.J., & Presno, I. (2014). Domestic and Foreign Announcements on Unconventional Monetary Policy and Exchange Rates. *Federal Reserve Bank of Boston Public Policy Briefs*, 13-7.

Draghi, M. (2014). Q&A session of September 04, 2014, *ECB Press Conference*, retrieved from: https://www.ecb.europa.eu/press/pressconf/2014/html/is140904.en.html.

Dunne, P., Everett, M., & Stuart, R. (2015). The Expanded Asset Purchase Programme – What, Why and How of Euro Area QE. In: Central Bank of Ireland: *Quarterly Bulletin 03 / July 15*, Dublin: Central Bank of Ireland.

Durbin, E., & Ng, D. (2005). The sovereign ceiling and emerging market corporate bond spreads. *Journal of International Money and Finance*, 24(2005), 631-649.

Durbin, J., & Koopman, S.J. (2001). *Time Series Analysis by State Space Methods*. Oxford and New York: Oxford University Press.

Ehlers, T., & Sushko, V. (2012). Unconventional Policies: Market Impact and Countervailing Factors. *BIS Quarterly Review*, September 2012, 6-7.

Eichert, F. (2014). A brave new world: Market reacts to final CBPP3 details. Retrieved on November 18, 2016 from http://nordic-fi.com/a-brave-new-world-market-reacts-to-final-cbpp3-details/#!prettyPhoto.

Ericsson, J., & Renault, O. (2006). Liquidity and Credit Risk. *The Journal of Finance*, 61(5), 2219-2250.

Eser, F., & Schwab, B. (2015). Evaluating the impact of unconventional monetary policy measures: Epirical evidence from the ECB's Securities Markets Programme. *Journal of Financial Economics*, 119, 147-167.

Eser, F., Amaro, M.C., Iacobelli, S., & Rubens, M. (2012). The Use of the Eurosystem's Monetary Policy Instruments and Operational Framework since 2009. *European Central Bank – Occasional Paper Series*, No 135.

European Banking Authority (2016). EBA Report on Covered Bonds. *EBA-Op-2016-23 | 20 December 2016*. Retrieved on February 14, 2017 from https://www.eba.europa.eu/documents/10180/1699643/EBA+Report+on+Covered+Bonds+(EBA-Op-2016-23).pdf.

European Central Bank (2008). Conduct of a special term refinancing operation. ECB Press Release, September 29, 2008.

European Central Bank (2009). Decision of the European Central Bank of 2 July 2009 on the implementation of the covered bond purchase program (ECB/2009/16). *Official Journal of the European Union*, L175.

European Central Bank (2010). Final Monthly Report on the Eurosystem's Covered Bond Purchase Programme. *European Central Bank*. June 2010.

European Central Bank (2011). Decision of the European Central Bank of 3 November 2011 on the implementation of the second covered bond purchase program (ECB/2011/17). *Official Journal of the European Union*, L297.

European Central Bank (2013). Details on securities holdings acquired under the Securities Markets Programme. Retrieved on February 13, 2017 from: https://www.ecb.europa.eu/press/pr/date/2013/html/pr130221_1.en.html

European Central Bank (2014). Decision of the European Central Bank of 15 October 2014 on the implementation of the third covered bond purchase program (ECB/2014/40). *Official Journal of the European Union*, L335.

European Central Bank (2015a). *Data on daily liquidity conditions*, retrieved on July 13, 2015 from https://www.ecb.europa.eu/stats/monetary/res/html/index.en.html.

European Central Bank (2015b). *FAQs on the Eurosystem's third covered bond purchase programme (CBPP3)*. Retrieved on November 10, 2016, from: https://www.ecb.europa.eu/mopo/implement/omt/html/cbpp3-qa.en.html.

European Central Bank (2016). *Breakdown of holdings under the CBPP3*. Retrieved on November 10, 2016, from: https://www.ecb.europa.eu/mopo/pdf/CBPP3_breakdown_history.csv?97369c6915bc0f84c6b20e7eef74587c.

European Central Bank (2017). Asset purchase programmes. Retrieved on 13 February 2017 from: https://www.ecb.europa.eu/mopo/implement/omt/html/index.en.html

European Covered Bond Council (2016). Statistics. In *2016 ECBC European Covered Bond Fact Book* (pp. 552-585).

European Stabilization Mechanism (2017). *Spain: a fast and effective programme*. Retrieved on February 14, 2017 from: https://www.esm.europa.eu/assistance/spain.

Falagiarda, M., & Reitz, S. (2015). Announcements of ECB Unconventional Programs: Implications for the Sovereign Spreads of Stressed Euro Area Countries. Journal of International Money and Finance, 53, 276-295.

Fawley, B.W., & Neely, C.J. (2013). Four Stories of Quantitative Easing. *Federal Reserve of St. Louis Review*, 95(1), 51-88.

Federal Reserve (2008). Press Release - Release Date: November 25, 2008, For release at 8:15 a.m. EST. Retrieved on February 13, 2017, from: https://www.federalreserve.gov/newsevents/press/monetary/20081125b.htm

Fratzscher, M., Lo Duca, M., & Straub, R. (2014). ECB unconventional monetary policy actions: Market impact, international spillovers and transmission channels. In Paper presented at the *15th Jacques Polak Annual Research Conference*, Washington, DC. International Monetary Fund.

Füss, R., & Zietz, J. (2016). The Economic Drivers of Differences in House Price Inflation Rate Across MSAs. *Journal of Housing Economics*, 31(1), 35-53.

Fuster, A., & Willen, P.S. (2010). $1.25 Trillion is Still Real Money: Some Facts About the Effects of the Federal Reserve's Mortgage Market Investments. *Federal Reserve Bank of Boston Public Policy Discussion papers*, 10-4.

Gabor, D. (2012). The power of collateral: the ECB and bank funding strategies in crisis. Working Paper.

Gagnon, J., Raskin, M., Remache, J., & Sack, B. (2011). Large-Scale Asset Purchases by the Federal Reserve: Did They Work? *FRBNY Economic Policy Review*, May 2011, 41-59.

Gerlach-Kristen, P. (2015). The impact of ECB crisis measures on euro-area CDS spreads. *Financial Markets and Portfolio Management*, 29, 149-168.

Gern, K.-J., Jansen, N., Kooths, S., & Wolters, M. (2015). Quantitative Easing in the Euro Area: Transmission Channels and Risks. *Intereconomics*, 2015(4), 206-212.

Gibson, H.D., Hall, S.G., & Tavlas, G.S. (2016). The effectiveness of the ECB's asset purchase programs of 2009 to 2012. *Journal of Macroeconomics*, 47, 45-57.

Glick, R., & Leduc, S. (2012). Central bank announcements of asset purchases and the impact on global financial and commodity markets. *Journal of International Money and Finance*, 31(8), 2078-2101.

Grande, G., Levy, A., Panetta, F., & Zaghini, A. (2011). Public guarantees on bank bonds: Effectiveness and distortions. *OECD Financial Market Trends*, 2011(2).

Grossmann, R., & Stöcker, O. (2016). Overview of Covered Bonds. In European Covered Bond Council, *2016 ECBC European Covered Bond Fact Book* (pp. 131-141).

Hamilton, J.D., & Wu, J.C. (2012). The Effectiveness of Alternative Monetary Policy in a Zero Lower Bound Environment. *Journal of Money, Credit and Banking*, Supplement to 44(1), 2-46.

Hancock, D., & Passmore, W. (2011). Did the Federal Reserve's MBS purchase program lower mortgage rates? *Journal of Monetary Economics*, 58(2011), 498-514.

Hannoun, H. (2012) Monetary Policy in the Crisis: Testing the Limits of Monetary Policy, Speech at *47th SEACEN Governors' Conference Seoul*, Korea, 13-14 February 2012.

Harvey, A. (1989). *Forecasting Structural Time Series Models and the Kalman Filter*. Cambridge University Press: Cambridge.

Harvey, A. (1997). Trends, Cycles, and Autoregressions. *Economic Journal*, 107, 192-201.

Hibbert, J., Kirchner, A., Kretzschmar, G., Li, R., & McNeil, A. (2009). Liquidity Premium – Literature review of theoretical and empirical evidence. Research Report, retrieved on February 14, 2017 from https://pdfs.semanticscholar.org/fa0c/3b83e0c9ddee13a0a9c69afb323425af2494.pdf.

Hillenbrand, F. (2013). Covered Bonds in der Insolvenz – ein systematischer Überblick. *Der langfristige Kredit*, 2013(14), 17-19.

Houben, A., & Slingenberg, J.W. (2013). Collateral scarcity and asset encumbrance: implications for the Euorpean financial system. In Banque de France (Eds.), *Financial Stability Review* (April 2013, pp. 197-206).

International Monetary Fund (2011). Germany: Technical Note on the Future of German Mortgage-Backed Covered Bond (Pfandbrief) and Securitization Markets. Country Report No. 11/369, *International Monetary Fund (IMF)*, Retrieved on February 14, 2017 from http://www.imf.org/external/pubs/ft/scr/2011/cr11369.pdf.

Jobst, A. (2015). Monetary Policy and Capital Market Integration in the Euro Area: What Is The Role of Covered Bonds? *The Journal of Structured Finance*, Winter 2015, 107-119.

Jobst, A., Kiff, J., & Spackman, C. (2009). *The Covered Bond Squeeze Play*. Retrieved on November 10, 2016 from: http://voxeu.org/debates/ commentaries/covered-bond-squeeze-play.

Joyce, M., Lasaosa, A., Stevens, I., & Tong, M. (2011).The financial market impact of quantitative easing in the United Kingdom. *International Journal of Central Banking*, 7(3), 113-161.

Kempf, A., Korn, O., & Uhrig-Homburg (2012). The term structure of illiquidity premia. *Journal of Banking & Finance*, 36, 1381-1391.

Kettemann, A., & Krogstrup, S. (2014). Portfolio balance effects of the SNB's bond purchase program. *Journal of Macroeconomics*, 40, 132-149.

Kilponen, J., Laakkonen, H., & Vilmunen, J. (2015). Sovereign Risk, European Crisis-Resolution Policies and Bond Spreads. *International Journal of Central Banking*, 11(2), 285-323.

Koulischer, F., & Struyven, D. (2014). Central bank liquidity provision and collateral quality. *Journal of Banking and Finance*, 49(2014), 113-130.

Koziol, C., & Sauerbier, P. (2007). Valuation of Bond Illiquidity – An Option-Theoretical Approach. *The Journal of Fixed Income*, Spring 2007, 81-107.

Krishnamurthy, A., & Vissing-Jorgensen, A. (2011). The Effects of Quantitative Easing on Interest Rates: Channels and Implications for Policy. *NBER Working Paper Series*, Working Paper 17555.

Krishnamurthy, A., Nagel, S., & Vissing-Jorgensen, A. (2014). ECB Policies involving Government Purchases: Impact and Channels. Working paper.

Kucharčuková, O.B., Claeys, P., & Vašíček, B. (2014). Spillover of the ECB's Monetary policy Outside the Euro Area: How Different is Conventional form Unconventional Policy?. *Working Paper Series 15*, Czeck National Bank.

Larsson, C.F. (2013). What did Frederick the great know about financial engineering? A survey of recent covered bond market developments and research. *North American journal of Economics and Finance*, 25(2013), 22-39.

Lenza, M., Pill, H., & Reichlin, L. (2010). Monetary Policy in Exceptional Times. *Working Paper Series No 1253*, European Central Bank.

Levy, A., & Schich, S. (2010). The design of government guarantees for bank bonds: Lessons from the recent financial crisis. *OECD Financial Market Trends*, 2010(2).

Longstaff, F.A., & Schwartz, E.S. (1995). A simple approach to valuing risky fixed and floating rate debt. *Journal of Finance*, 50 (3), 789–819.

Loutskina, E. (2011). The role of securitization in bank liquidity and funding management. *Journal of Financial Economics*, 100(3), 663-684.

Martin-Oliver, A., & Saurina, J. (2007). Why do banks securitize assets? Working paper.

Melm, M., Rudolf, F., & Schuller, M. (2016). Covered Bond Purchase Programme 3: Implications for primary and secondary markets. In European Covered Bond Council, *2016 ECBC European Covered Bond Fact Book* (pp. 41-52).

Mishkin, F.S. (1996). The Channels of Monetary Transmission: Lessons for Monetary Policy. *NBER Working Paper*, 5464.

Neely, C.J. (2015). Unconventional monetary policy had large international effects. *Journal of Banking and Finance*, 52, 101-111.

Packer, F., Stever, R., & Upper, C. (2007). The Covered Bond Market. *BIS Quarterly Review*, September 2007, 43-55.

Packmohr, T., & Weigerding, M. (2015). CBPP3: The ECB's third covered bond purchase programme. *Der Pfandbrief*, 20, 20-27.

Pattipeilohy, C., End van den, J.W., Tabbae, M., Frost, J., & Haan de, J. (2013). Unconventional Monetary Policy of the ECB during the Financial Crisis: An Assessment and New Evidence. *Working Paper No. 381*, De Nederlandsche Bank.

Peersman, G. (2011). Macroeconomic effects of unconventional monetary policy in the Euro area. *Working Paper Series 1397*, European Central Bank.

Pelagatti, M.M. (2015). *Time Series Modelling with Unobserved Components*. London: Chapman.

Perraudin., W. (2014). Covered Bonds versus ABS Liquidity: A Comment on EBA's Proposed HQLA Definition. *afme Briefing Notes*.

Prokopczuk, M., & Vonhoff, V. (2012). Risk Premia in Covered Bond Markets. *Journal of Fixed Income,* 22(2), 19-29.

Prokopczuk, M., Siewert, J.B., & Vonhoff, V. (2013). Credit Risk in Covered Bonds. *Journal of Empirical Finance*, 21, 102-120.

Price Waterhouse Coopers (2012). Uncovering Covered Bonds. Retrieved on February 14, 2017 from https://www.pwc.com/gx/en/banking-capital-markets/assets/pwc-uncovering-covered-bonds.pdf.

Quirk, P. (2010). Cover Me: The Economy Is on Fire (The German Pfandbrief). *German Law Journal*, 11(12), 1324-1346.

Ricci, O. (2014). The impact of monetary policy announcements on the stock price of large European banks during the financial crisis. *Journal of Banking and Finance*, 52, 245-255.

Rivolta, G. (2014). An Event Study Analysis of ECB Unconventional Monetary Policy, *Working Paper n. 201-02*, University of Milan.

Rogers, J.H., Sotti, C., & Wright, J.H. (2014). Evaluating Asset-Market Effects of Unconventional Monetary Policy: A Cross-Country Comparison. *Board of Governors of the Federal Reserve System International Finance Discussion Papers*, 1101

Roll, R. (1984). A Simple Implicit Measure of the Effective Bid-Ask Spread in an Efficient Market. *Journal of Finance*, 39(4), 1127-1139.

Rudolf, F., & Rühlmann, K. (2016). Extendable maturity structures – the new normal? In European Covered Bond Council, *2016 ECBC European Covered Bond Fact Book* (pp. 41-52).

Sachs, J. (2012). We Must Look Beyond Keynes to Fix Our Problems, *Financial Times*, December 18, 2012, 9.

Sarafana, J. (2012). Focus on Peripheral Economies: Input Factors for Covered Bond Spreads and ECB Purchase Programme. In European Covered Bond Council, *2012 ECBC European Covered Bond Fact Book* (pp. 47-52).

Schäfer, H., & Hochstein, M. (1999). Competitiveness of the German Pfandbrief. Recent theoretical and empirical findings. *Kredit & Kapital*, 34 (4), 547–580.

Schuster, P., & Uhrig-Homburg, M. (2015). Limits to arbitrage and the term structure of bond illiquidity premiums. *Journal of Banking & Finance, 57*, 143-159.

Schwarcz, S.L. (2011). The Condrum of Covered Bonds, *The Business Lawyer*, 66(May 2011), 561-586.

Spangler, M. & Werner, R. (2014). German Covered Bonds – Overview and Risk Analysis of Pfandbriefe. In *Springer Briefs in Finance*.

Stöcker, O. (2014). Fundamental questions on covered bond legal frameworks from a European perspective. *Housing Finance International*, Winter 2014, 28-32.

Stroebel, J.C., & Taylor, J.B. (2009). Estimated Impact of the Fed's Mortgage-Backed Securities Purchase Program. *NBER Working Paper Series*, 15626.

Swanson, E.T. (2011). *Let's Twist Again: a High-Frequency Event-Study Analysis of Operation Twist and Its Implications for QE2*. Brookings Papers on Economic Activity.

Swiss National Bank (2009). Monetary policy assessment of 12 March 2009. *Press release of March 12, 2009*.

Szczerbowicz, U. (2015). The ECB's unconventional monetary policies: Have they lowered market borrowing costs for banks and governments? *International Journal of Central Banking*, 11(4), 91-127.

Volk, B., & Hillenbrand, F. (2006). The European Jumbo covered bond Market in the Footsteps of the German Pfandbrief. *Der Pfandbrief*, 11, 58-70.

Watfe, G. (2015). The Impact of the ECB's Asset Purchase Programmes on Sovereign Bond Spreads in the Euro Area. *Bruges European Economic Research Papers*, 35/2015.

Will, F. (2009). Covered Bonds and Repo. In European Covered Bond Council, *2009 ECBC European Covered Bond Fact Book* (pp. 27-37).

Winkler, B. (2009). The Pfandbrief Market 2009/2010. In Association of German Pfandbrief Banks, *The Pfandbrief 2009|2010* (14th ed., pp. 24-35).

Zietz, J., & Traian, A. (2014). When was the U.S. Housing Downturn Predictable? A Comparison of Univariate Forecasting Methods. *Quarterly Review of Economics and Finance*, 54(2), 271-281.

Appendix

Appendix 1: Goals of CBPP1 to CBPP3

Goals of CBPP1: “The objectives of these purchases are to contribute to: (a) promoting the ongoing decline in money market term rates; (b) easing funding conditions for credit institutions and enterprises; (c) encouraging credit institutions to maintain and expand their lending to clients; and (d) improving market liquidity in important segments of the private debt securities market.” (ECB, 2009)

Goals of CBPP2: “The objectives of the second program are to contribute to: (a) easing funding conditions for credit institutions and enterprises; and (b) encouraging credit institutions to maintain and expand lending to their clients.” (ECB, 2011)

Goals of CBPP3: “Alongside the ABS purchase program (ABSPP) and the Targeted Longer-Term Refinancing Operations (TLTROs) (1), the CBPP3 will further enhance the transmission of monetary policy, facilitate credit provision to the euro area economy, generate positive spill-overs to other markets and, as a result, ease the ECB's monetary policy stance, and contribute to a return of inflation rates to levels closer to 2%.” (ECB, 2014)

H. Markmann, *Covered Bonds under Unconventional Monetary Policy*,
Essays in Real Estate Research 14,
https://doi.org/10.1007/978-3-658-20975-9

Appendix 2: Unit Root Test

Table 23: Dickey-Fuller Test for Unit Roots

	(42) EUR	(43) GER	(44) FRA	(45) ESP	(46) IRL
Test Statistic (Z(t))	-0.580	-0.455	-0.385	-0.786	-0.897
MacKinnon appr. p-value for Z(t)	0.8755	0.9005	0.9126	0.8231	0.7891
Observations	494	494	494	494	494

The observation period is January 2, 2006 to July 3, 2015. Significance levels: * 0.10, ** 0.05, *** 0.01.

Kolibri 360 GmbH
Ferdinand-Jühlke-Straße 7
99095 Erfurt, Deutschland
produktsicherheit@kolibri360.de